7 DAY
BOOK

# Psychosomatic Health

## The Body and the Word

**Maggie Turp**

*Consultant Editor:* Jo Campling

palgrave

First published 2001 by
PALGRAVE
Houndmills, Basingstoke, Hampshire RG21 6XS and
175 Fifth Avenue, New York, N.Y. 10010
Companies and representatives throughout the world

PALGRAVE is the new global academic imprint of
St. Martin's Press LLC Scholarly and Reference Division and
Palgrave Publishers Ltd (formerly Macmillan Press Ltd).

ISBN 0–333–79193–2 hardback
ISBN 0–333–79194–0 paperback

This book is printed on paper suitable for recycling and made from fully managed and sustained forest sources.

A catalogue record for this book is available from the British Library.

Editing and origination by
Aardvark Editorial, Mendham, Suffolk

10   9   8   7   6   5   4   3   2   1
10  09  08  07  06  05  04  03  02  01

Printed in China

*For Joe and Frankie,*
*who showed me how to play*

# Contents

# Preface

For many children growing up in the 1950s, the physical dangers and economic insecurities of the War seemed to cast a long shadow. My own childhood experience was of a certain level of anxiety, a feeling that constant vigilance was required in order to fend off unnamed dangers. Life was busy, well organised and often enjoyable, but a sense of constraint remained, epitomised in my mother's frequent caution that 'It will end in tears.' 'It' could refer to almost anything that was physically exuberant, from climbing a tree to a pillow fight with my sister.

Exploring a wider range of physical experiences, which I could also describe as exploring a wider range of experiences of myself, has formed part of a personal journey which has involved me in many different activities. I have been involved in bodywork and psychoanalytic psychotherapy, yoga, massage, Alexander technique, playing tennis and playing boisterous games with my own children. The understanding that health is 'psychosomatic', that health and recovery involve both physical and psychological aspects of the self, is firmly embedded within my own experience. My work as a psychotherapist has offered the opportunity to supplement personal experience with the experiences of others.

Through my work, I have learned that an illness with a psychological label, such as depression, almost always has a physical counterpart, for example physical lethargy or muscular weakness. In the same way, a physically produced phenomenon, such as prolonged post-operative pain, has psychological consequences for the individual.

There is no shortage of books or professional papers concerning the interaction of the physical and the psychological in cases of illness and difficulty. However, very little has been written on this same theme where health and recovery are concerned. I intend that this book should go some way towards filling the gap that I discovered when I began my exploration of the psychosomatic processes that underpin and enhance health.

Prior to becoming a psychotherapist, I worked in psychology, social work, youth work, adult education and gardening! I hope that this diversity of professional experience has helped me to write a book which, although it wrestles with complex psychoanalytic and philosophical issues, is nevertheless accessible to a wide variety of readers.

# Acknowledgements

A first-time author is fortunate if she finds a helpful and encouraging publisher, and it has been a great pleasure to work with Palgrave. Special thanks go to Jo Campling, who commissioned the book.

I am grateful to all the people who have shared their stories with me, including friends and clients. Without them, there would have been no book. I decided at the outset not to interfere with the psychotherapy process by asking clients for permission to write about their experiences. Instead, I have opted to construct clinical case studies from a variety of real incidents and interactions. The reader may be disappointed to know that 'Richard', 'Linda', 'Betty' and 'Sheila' do not exist as 'real people', but client confidentiality has been my paramount concern.

Special thanks are due to the families who allowed me into their homes to observe infants and children and who gave me permission to share these observations with a wider audience; and, of course, to the babies themselves for their demonstration of the art of just being. In the observation extracts, only the biographical details of children and families have been changed. I also greatly appreciated the opportunity to observe at 'Baby Massage' and 'Baby Gym' classes run by Peter Walker at the Active Birth Centre in London.

Many of the ideas for this book emerged during a period of study at the Tavistock Clinic, where the thoughtful and stimulating teaching added breadth and depth to my understanding of psycho-analytic theory and practice. My tutor, Dr Meira Likierman, assisted me in making links between my own ideas and those embedded within existing psychoanalytic theory and encouraged me to seek publication. The staff at the Department of Health and Social Care, University of Hertfordshire, have shown considerable generosity, both in allowing me the time to write and in their ongoing support for my work. Dr Julia Buckroyd, Director of Studies for Counselling, read the entire text in draft and has been particularly encouraging. Successive cohorts of students on the MA Module in Psychosomatics at the University of Hertfordshire played a role in the evolution of the book, and I thank them for the generosity and enthusiasm that they have brought to our sessions together.

I wish to acknowledge as well the role played by my long-suffering tennis coach, yoga teacher, psychotherapist and massage therapist, all of whom have helped me towards a better understanding of my own state of 'psychosomatic indwelling'. I also want to thank my women friends, with whom I have shared many walking holidays, Terry in Germany and my children Joe and Frankie, who taught me a great deal about the enjoyment of physicality.

Writing a book for psychotherapy practitioners, for professionals in allied fields such as social work, psychology and medicine and for readers whose interest in health and parenting is personal rather than professional is a particular kind of undertaking. If I have avoided some of the pitfalls, it is largely thanks to my friends and colleagues, especially Caroline Dalal, Ced Jackson, Val Richards and Jane Sufian, each of whom commented on the book or on a part of the book from a broad health and social services perspective. Finally, very special thanks to my husband, Phil Leask, for the long walks, for the conversations late into the night, and for taking time out from his own writing to comment on each chapter in the role of 'intelligent lay reader'.

Certain chapters in this book draw on prior publications of the author. The author and the publisher gratefully acknowledge permission from the following journals to reprint passages of previously published material.

Chapter 1: 'In sickness and in health? Psychoanalysis and psycho-somatics', *Psychodynamic Counselling*, **4**(1): 3–16, 1998; Chapter 7: 'Touch, enjoyment and health: in infancy', *European Journal of Psychotherapy, Counselling and Health*, **2**(1): 19–35, 1999; Chapter 10: 'Touch, enjoyment and health: in adult life', *European Journal of Psychotherapy, Counselling and Health*, **3**(1): 61–76, 2000; Chapter 11: 'The role of physical exercise in emotional well-being', *Psychodynamic Counselling*, **3**(2): 165–77, 1997; Chapter 12: 'Working with body storylines', *Psychodynamic Counselling*, **5**(3): 301–17, 1999.

The above journals are published by Routledge, Taylor & Francis Ltd; http://www/tandf.co.uk/journals/routledge/13642537.html

# Part I

## Narratives of Health

# CHAPTER 1

# Introduction

*This book is written for the very large number of people who take a serious interest, whether personal or professional, in the interplay of psychological and physical aspects of health. It brings a psychoanalytic perspective to bear on our many and varied experiences and uses of physicality. Chapter 1 introduces the key themes that will be explored in the pages that follow.*

## The body and the word

In the beginning, the word is just one aspect of bodily experience. To the newborn infant, it is all cadence, rhythm, volume and tone. Words soothe, tease, excite or shock; sustain or cut across the infant's own sense of its being. At this stage, the meaning of words resides in their physical impact alone. Later, words are understood to have a representational value also. If I say to a friend, 'Look! The cat has come in', the words themselves have a meaning. But the physicality of the words remains crucial to a more complete understanding. It is the manner of my delivery, and that alone, which will reveal whether the cat is an accursed nuisance or a loved and welcomed family member. Some playwrights – Harold Pinter springs to mind – are exquisitely aware of the physical impact of words. They create characters who use words as piercing darts, as weapons of war, who call into question our understanding of words as a civilised and refined form of communication.

The 'word', as I use the term here, includes not only speech and text, but also the whole quasi-verbal activity of thinking. The age of dualism, usually acknowledged as beginning with the work of philosopher René Descartes (1596–1650), has seen the body located in a separate arena from the word. In Cartesian philosophy, thinking is attributed to the 'mind', which is seen as distinct from the body. Within holistic perspectives, this separation is disputed. Thinking and speaking are seen as aspects of our overall functioning, which is rooted in our ever-present embodiment. The body is regarded as essentially communicative and replete with memory and meaning. Our fingers remember the number of the bicycle padlock. Our bodies remember how to ride the bicycle, even after ten years, twenty years, out of the saddle.

The psychoanalyst and paediatrician D.W. Winnicott (1896–1971), who will be referred to on many occasions as the book proceeds, conceptualised the psyche-soma as a *unity*. In his work, 'mind' or mental functioning is described as being no more than a 'special case of the functioning of the psyche-soma' (Winnicott, 1949a). Like Winnicott, I believe that the nature of our being is essentially psychosomatic, in the original meaning of the word, given in the *Concise Oxford English Dictionary* (9th edn, 1995) as 'of mind and body together'.

As most readers will be aware, psychoanalysis has been involved with psychosomatics from the very start. It was Freud who developed and made famous the 'talking cure' to help patients with a variety of physical symptoms which had not responded to conventional medical treatments. The array of symptoms in question was extraordinary – nervous tics, paralysed limbs, an inability to drink water, sexual dysfunction, outbursts of speaking in a foreign language accompanied by an inability to speak in one's native language. For the most part, the term 'psychosomatic' has continued to be used, as Freud used it, in relation to situations involving pathology. We are accustomed to seeing the phrases 'psychosomatic illness', 'psychosomatic symptom' and 'psychosomatic disorder' but not the phrase 'psychosomatic health'.

In this book, I characterise health in all its aspects as 'psychosomatic', as involving a complex and ongoing interplay of physiological and psychological factors. I build on the psychoanalytic understanding that, as a part of our ongoing human meaning-making activity, we consciously and unconsciously imbue our physical experiences with psychological significance. I suggest that the meanings that we ascribe to our experiences of physicality are woven into a narrative, which I have called a 'body storyline' (Turp, 1999a). It follows that physical changes are mirrored in psychological changes and vice versa. For example, it may be the experience of a new sense of physical energy that indicates that emotional recovery is under way.

A client who came to me for psychotherapy had been depressed for more than a year, following a very harrowing sequence of events. One day, she found herself wanting to go for a walk. Rather excitedly, she dug out her boots from the cupboard under the stairs. She said to them 'Hello there. I'm sorry I left you in that musty cupboard for such a long time.' Then she put them on and went for a long hike. She told me that while she was walking, she began to feel much better. In fact, she felt really healthy. I asked her what it meant to feel healthy. She thought for a long time and then said that for the first time in ages she was able to imagine some kind of a future.

## Postmodern themes in psychoanalytic thinking

The style and content of this book reflect the growing influence of a postmodern perspective. The overlaps and interstices between psychoanalysis and postmodernism have seen Freud's work profoundly reshaped in the body of writing contributed by French psychoanalyst Jaques Lacan and his colleagues. More subtle and diffuse effects of postmodernism have found expression in a shift away from 'totalising' theories of supposedly universal application. Description and observation have come to the fore, and the local and provisional nature of 'truths' is more widely accepted. As a part of this development, psychoanalytic infant observation has become an important tool for understanding the nature of our experience. In psychoanalytic infant observation, description takes precedence over theory and the coexistence of multiple 'versions' or interpretations of the same observation is an accepted part of the discussion.

Winnicott spoke in favour of observation before these shifts in thinking took hold. His phenomenological approach and his desire to keep the consideration of physicality at the centre of proceedings offer a secure base for thinking about psychosomatic health. Winnicott accorded an unusual degree of attention in both his practice and his writing to the physical 'handling' aspects of the mother's care of the infant, and to the ongoing adult issue of the 'indwelling of the psyche in the soma' (Winnicott, 1970). Other writers have also noted his distinctive emphasis on the *physicality* of the self:

> (But) in post World War Two developments, psychoanalysis has become primarily a theory of mind and mental contents. Winnicott's work stands out from this tendency in the deeply physical sense that he conveys to us about his work and his understanding of mental processes. (Orbach, 1995: 3)

Winnicott was also unusual in his explicit concern with health as well as with illness. In *The Spontaneous Gesture*, which draws together many of Winnicott's letters to other analysts, Rodman writes of Winnicott that:

> His theory of health is not defined as the absence of pathology. He is interested in more than that. He wants to define a healthy life in positive terms. (Rodman, 1987: xix)

Alongside Winnicott's work, I draw on a narrative perspective, which represents one line of development of the postmodern ethos. My sources include the work of American psychoanalyst Roy Schafer and of Australian family therapists David White and Michael Epson. The basic narrative assumption in play is that events and experiences are available to us only as 'versions' and that we have no direct access to the true and the real. In an area of discourse which has spawned many dense and difficult texts, Schafer expresses this idea with admirable clarity:

> It is especially important to emphasize that narrative is not an alternative to truth or reality; rather it is the mode in which, inevitably, truth and reality are presented. We have only versions of the true and the real. (1992: xiv)

This point of view has profound implications for psychotherapy practice. It speaks of the impossibility of neutrality, implying that all behaviour, including the psychotherapy dialogue, is organised and constrained both by the immediate context in which it is performed and by the wider social and political context inhabited by psychotherapist and client. Recognising the inevitable influence of consciously or unconsciously held beliefs or assumptions leads to an approach characterised by curiosity, by a greater respect for

the client's way of seeing, by the exploration of alternative possibilities and hypotheses. The idea of arriving at a final truth, to the
exclusion of other versions of events, falls by the wayside.
Reflecting on his own psychoanalytic practice, Schafer states:

> Psychoanalysis is conducted as a dialogue. In this dialogue, actions and
> happenings (for example, traumatic events) are continuously being
> told by the analysand and sooner or later retold interpretively by both
> analyst and analysand. Closure is always provisional to allow for further
> retellings. (1992: xv)

As will emerge, it has served my purpose to create an interface
between Winnicott's work and narrative theory. Would Winnicott
have wanted this interface to be created? It is, of course, impossible
to know, but it is clear that Winnicott was not afraid to voice his
opposition to orthodox thinking. His independence of thought is
revealed in his refusal to align himself with either Melanie Klein's
followers or Anna Freud's followers during the 1940s, and in his
sometimes sharply critical letters to members of the Kleinian group
of the British Psychoanalytic Society during the 1950s.

It seems to me too that Winnicott's work has a great deal in
common with the concerns of postmodernism. Winnicott found
himself intuitively opposed to 'totalising' tendencies. He favoured
observation and description over attempts to construct a grand
overarching theory. He had no desire to see everything 'sewn up'.
When Joan Rivière wrote, in the preface to Klein's text *Developments
in Psychoanalysis* (1952), that Klein had produced:

> an *integrated* theory which, though still in outline, nevertheless takes
> account of all the psychical manifestations, normal and abnormal, from
> birth to death, and leaves no unbridgeable gulfs and no phenomena
> outstanding without intelligible relation to the rest.

Winnicott vehemently expressed his opposition. He sent a letter to
Melanie Klein stating that:

> You are the only one who can destroy this language called the Kleinian
> doctrine and Kleinianism and all that with a constructive aim. If you do
> not destroy it then this artificially integrated phenomenon must be
> attacked destructively. (Rodman, 1987: xxii)

In relation to practice, Winnicott emphasised the importance of the facilitating environment, of the play, or interplay, between client and psychotherapist, of the transitional space between two people, the site of unconscious to unconscious communication and the crucible for the co-construction and reconstruction of experience. In his clinical work as well as in his public communications, Winnicott was concerned that theory – both in the narrow sense of personal beliefs and assumptions, and in the broader sense of psychoanalytic theories – should come into the service of practice, and not the other way round. He understood that theory had the potential to become a straitjacket and to stifle the creativity of therapist and client alike.

All of the above applies also to those analysts who have drawn on and developed Winnicott's work – Jan Abram, Michael Balint, Christopher Bollas, Patrick Casement, Ronald Fairbairn, Masud Khan, Marion Milner, Adam Phillips, Charles Rycroft, Thomas Ogden, Val Richards, Neville Symington and many others. In recent years, a fruitful dialogue has developed between the Kleinian and the British Independent strands within psychoanalysis. In the sphere of psychoanalytic infant observation, for example, Winnicott's understandings are thoughtfully integrated with those of the post-Kleinians. I have found that this conjunction offers a particularly rich blend of ways of seeing.

The practice of psychoanalysis has always taken the form of narrative and dialogue, of a certain kind of conversation between two individuals. Adam Phillips has described psychoanalysis as 'a story and a way of telling stories that makes some people feel better' (1993: xvii). For a long time, however, there was no readily available philosophical context within which to locate this central narrative and conversational aspect of the psychotherapy process. Postmodernism has provided that context and in so doing has faced psychoanalysis with a challenge. In some quarters, psychoanalytic orthodoxy continues to hold sway. This orthodoxy reveals itself in an unquestioning approach to basic assumptions. Psychoanalytic concepts continue to be discussed as if they were solid 'facts', certain and unchanging realities which hold good in all cultures and all circumstances. In other quarters, though, there is an openness to and engagement with postmodern ideas, particularly the ideas of social constructionism and cultural relativism.

Messer and Warren (1995) set out the central issue raised by contemporary developments in the following manner:

> The question is raised as to whether good psychotherapy entails the discernment and working through of the correct and accurate underlying focus or conflict – which derives from a modernist, logical positivist perspective – or whether it is more like story construction or meaning making – an idea more wedded to a postmodern outlook. (1995: viii)

## The 'joining up' of physical and psychological experience

The book falls into three parts, and my hope is that they do join up and form some kind of coherent whole. The first part is concerned with broad historical and contemporary issues which inform our understanding of the bodymind question. The second draws on psychoanalytic infant observations and considers how a sense of psychosomatic unity evolves and is supported, and at the same time how it can be damaged or depleted. The third section looks at the question of the recovery and enhancement of psychosomatic health, drawing on examples from psychodynamic counselling and psychoanalytic psychotherapy practice. A theme that links together the three parts of the book is the process described by Winnicott in terms of the joining up of the physical and psychological aspects of experience, first played out by the mother with her baby:

> The beginning of that part of the baby's development which I am calling personalization, or which can be described as an indwelling of the psyche in the soma, is to be found in the mother's ability to join up her emotional involvement, which is originally physical and physiological. (Winnicott, 1970: 264)

In ordinary 'good enough' circumstances, the mother-to-be first engages in this joining up within herself, moving from seeing herself as simply 'pregnant' to feeling herself to be in relationship to an unborn child, with personal characteristics of his or her own. Stroking the infant in the womb through the skin of the abdomen, attributing intentions to the unborn infant ('I see you're in no mood to let me have a sleep!') and asking questions ('How are you doing in there? Is it getting a bit squashed, eh?') are some of the external markers of this shift. After the birth, this ability to 'join up' is communicated to the infant through maternal care which involves a seamless experience of being held in mind and physically handled. Winnicott suggests that maternal handling meets with and supports an inborn tendency within the infant towards integration. Adam Phillips offers the following summary:

> This natural 'tendency to integrate' is made possible by the mother's care in which the infant is 'kept warm, handled and bathed and rocked and named'. (1988: 78)

The question of how the mental and physical facets of experience are joined up is the 'connective tissue' (to use a body metaphor) which links together the three parts of the book. So it is that in Part I, I consider this joining up at the most general and abstract level, as it finds expression in changing historical and philosophical perspectives on the question of 'mind' and 'body'. In Part II, I illustrate and discuss the role of maternal handling in the individual infant's joining up of mental and physical facets of his experience and of himself. And in Part III, I consider adult narratives that reveal a need to address difficulties in feeling joined up, in feeling all of a piece within a skin. Here, the focus is on the psychotherapist's role in assisting a process of joining up, through the creation of a context which supports the establishment or restoration of 'a psyche-soma that lives and works in harmony with itself' (Winnicott, 1967: 29).

## Different approaches in health research

Many readers will be familiar with the well-established links between health, illness and social indices such as housing and income level. Research into health inequalities between different social and ethnic groups is of great importance and is indispensable to large-scale planning. I have not tried to summarise the research into the psychosocial aspects of health in this book, partly because my expertise is limited and partly because good summaries are available elsewhere (see, for example, Bakal, 1999; Sheridan and Radmacher, 1992).

I will say, however, that a full understanding of inequalities in health depends not only on identifying the key external factors, but also on understanding how individuals interpret their experience of an environment. Why does one person remain healthy in a disadvantaged situation while another falls ill? How does a low income translate into poor health at the level of the individual? It is in considering these questions from the point of view of the experiencing subject engaged in bringing meaning to his or her experiences that psychoanalytic thinking can make a valuable contribution. The point is not to arrive at general laws of connection between circumstances and individual health, *but rather to understand what it is like for an individual child or adult to sustain, to lose, or to recover a state of health.*

The psychoanalytic methodologies of the infant observation study and the clinical case study are those which I have used in my original research. They are described at the beginning of Parts II and III of the book respectively. At certain points, I have also introduced findings from quantitative research. In discussing the role of touch experiences in infancy, for example, I draw on several larger-scale studies to provide 'triangulation' (Denzin, 1970) of the qualitative evidence that I have gathered myself.

Within the general framework of factors that contribute to or detract from health, I have taken a particular interest in a more specific question. How are experiences of *touch* and *movement* implicated in the establishment, maintenance and recovery of health? Winnicott draws particular attention to these matters in his account of maternal handling, and I have extended his thinking to bring it into relation to 'self-handling' in adult life. The concept of self-handling, as I use it here, refers to *all* the experiences of movement and touch that we consciously or unconsciously seek out and that form a part of our continuously evolving body storylines.

## Outline of the book

In Chapter 2, I describe in more detail Winnicott's concept of 'the indwelling of the psyche in the soma'. I sketch out some key characteristics of a psychoanalytic approach to health and these are compared and contrasted in Chapter 3 with other holistic perspectives. Chapter 4 reviews key features of the biomedical model of health and looks at the relationship between science, philosophy and our understanding of health. Chapter 5 concludes Part I of the book, with a broad (although inevitably incomplete) overview of some specific psychoanalytic perspectives on 'mind and body' and/or 'embodied mind'.

Parts II and III of the book establish its character as a book of single cases, of individual narratives which I refer to as 'body story-lines' (Turp, 1999a). The examples illustrate some of the ways in which an individual comes to inhabit, experience and express his or her physicality. In both of these sections of the book, narratives of touch and movement experiences are at the centre of the discussion.

The infant observation section offers what is, as far as I am aware, the most sustained descriptive account available of 'handling' in infancy. The discussion focuses particularly on phys-ical aspects of maternal care, on the infant's self-initiated move-ments and on the responses encountered by the infant as he begins to become mobile. In my view, it is infant observation which makes the most compelling case for the essential unity of the psyche-soma. I have been fortunate in having permission from the families concerned to use observation extracts in their original form in the book, and only names and other identifying details have been changed.

The narratives in Part III come from clinical work, undertaken by myself or by psychotherapists and counsellors whom I supervise. In these cases, details have been changed, interspersed and re-compiled so that no one person will find his or her story revealed to the public eye. This part of the book considers individual endeavours to sustain and/or recover a sense of well-being, partic-ularly where poor handling in infancy or later trauma has damaged the psychosomatic integrity that underpins the experience of overall health.

I use the terms 'psychotherapist' and 'psychoanalyst' in the book as seems appropriate. What I have to say applies equally to psycho-dynamic counsellors, whose work is also represented here. Where a practitioner is working from a non-psychoanalytic perspective, for example family therapy, cognitive behavioural psychotherapy or a bodywork approach, I make this clear in the text. I use the word 'client' to refer to the person who is seeking help or self-understanding. For the sake of simplicity, the person mothering an infant is referred to throughout as 'the mother'. This person is most often the biological mother but may also be the father, a same-sex partner or a close family friend or relative. Infants are generally referred to as 'he', except where I am writing about a specific girl infant or where the gender of the infant makes a significant difference to the dynamic being described.

The book moves from some general and quite complex scene-setting to individual examples, taking the form of illustrative material written in non-technical language. Some readers may prefer to turn to this illustrative material first, and I have set the book out with this possibility in mind. Readers with a strong interest in infant development will probably feel inclined to begin with Part II, while those who are most interested in clinical work with adults may wish to move directly to Part III. The reader can return to the historical, theoretical and philosophical issues addressed in Part I at any stage.

# CHAPTER 2

# Psychoanalysis and Health

Let us say that in health a man or a woman is able to reach towards an identification with society without too great a loss of individual or personal impulse. (Winnicott, 1966: 112)

*This chapter outlines some of the characteristics specific to a psychoanalytic approach to health and physicality. As well as sketching out a general background, it introduces the two key themes, which form the framework of thinking for the book. They are D.W. Winnicott's concept of 'psychosomatic indwelling' and my own concept of 'body storylines', which resides at the interface between Winnicott's work and a narrative perspective.*

## The myth of perfect health

Lives dominated by impossible ideals – complete honesty, absolute knowledge, perfect happiness, eternal love – are lives experienced as continuous failure. (Phillips, 1999: 115)

Psychoanalysis has spoken consistently of the need to accept the mixed nature of both internal and external worlds, of the need to relinquish the idea of perfectibility. It is this, perhaps more than any other characteristic, which distinguishes it from humanistic approaches, some of which are explicitly opposed to the idea of limitation. The clash of perspectives to which I am referring emerges in the correspondence between the founding father of humanistic psychotherapy, Carl Rogers, and existential psychoanalyst, Rollo May. Rogers describes human beings as *'essentially* constructive in their fundamental nature, but damaged by their experience' (Kirschenbaum and Land Henderson, 1990: 238).

Elsewhere, Rogers outlines a bright vision of the future, as individuals break free of the evil influences of culture:

> This new world will be more and more humane. ...Its technology will be aimed at the enhancing, rather than the exploitation of persons and nature. It will release creativity, as individuals sense their power, their capacities, their freedom. (Kirschenbaum and Land Henderson, 1990: 356)

Rollo May responds by asking:

> But who is responsible for this destructive influence and injustice, except you and me and people like us? The culture is not something made up by fate and foisted upon us. (Kirschenbaum and Land Henderson, 1990: 241)

May's conclusion is the psychoanalytic conclusion of the human being as a creature of mixed potentials:

> These potentialities, driven by the daimonic urge, are the source both of our constructive and our destructive impulses. ...I propose that the evil in our culture is also the reflection of evil in ourselves, and vice versa. (Kirschenbaum and Land Henderson, 1990: 241)

From a psychoanalytic point of view, myths of perfectibility can be seen to exert a particular kind of tyranny over the individual. The myth of perfect health fuels acts of self-denial and self-punishment that carry an ever-increasing personal cost. Adam Phillips has called our attention back to Freud's understanding of unrealisable ideals as:

> refuges that stop us living in the world as it is and finding out what it is like, and therefore what we could be like in it. (Phillips, 1999: 17)

In relation to health, we need to think carefully about what is possible and liveable. It is perhaps no more than our immediate awareness and intermittent enjoyment of shifting experiences of energy, resilience and a desire for action, or of fatigue, weakness and a desire for rest. It is certainly the case that, along with the other animal species, we will succumb from time to time to illness and disease. That is, as Phillips puts it, 'what it is like'. It is not a matter of personal control or responsibility but rather one of the givens of our existence. We may well consider ourselves fortunate to live in an era when developments in medicine and improvements in public health have increased our life expectancy and decreased the amount of physical pain we are likely to suffer. But we are still mortal beings. Attrition, illness or accident will have the final say.

This is by no means to deny the reality of physical enjoyment, whether in making love, giving or receiving a massage, climbing a stiff hill, playing a sport or simply sitting and feeling well embodied, at home within one's own physicality. But to the extent that people insist on defining health as a permanent and complete absence of illness, or as a perfect state of well-being, they necessarily compromise such enjoyment. Difficulties are placed in the path of 'living in the world as it is'.

Clinical encounters with this situation are not uncommon. We find ourselves with people who seem almost entirely unable to enjoy their physicality. They harshly chastise themselves for all their imperfections, including their imperfect body shape and their occasional ailments. They 'admit' that they are at fault, telling us about their lapsed exercise programme, or diet, or vitamin regime, or blaming themselves for having drunk a glass or two of wine. They live lives that are constantly constrained and inhibited by fear and guilt. Sometimes, frustrated by their inability to care for themselves perfectly, they give up altogether and spiral down into gross self-indulgence, self-neglect or self-abuse. Their repeated failure to achieve the impossible ideal of perfect health is more than they can bear.

## Psychoanalysis and embodiment

Where psychosomatic illness is concerned, psychoanalysis has already shed a great deal of light on the interplay of physicality on the one hand and mental and emotional functioning on the other. Many renowned psychoanalysts have been involved in this work. Among them, Joyce McDougall's contribution merits particular mention. As I have already remarked, Freud's patients suffered from an extraordinary array of tics, coughs, paralyses, phobias and physical inhibitions. These symptoms, in all their colourful variety,

had defied the interventions of conventional medicine, yet they
yielded to the therapeutic effects of the 'talking cure'.

The interplay of psychosomatic processes in recovery and in the
enjoyment of health has been the subject of considerably less
research. There are, of course, reasons for this. The psychoanalyst
Charles Rycroft has written that:

> Psychoanalysis began as a branch of medicine and its raw material still
> derives from people who are in trouble and seeking help; it has there-
> fore more to say about illness than about health, and a tendency to
> describe human nature in a terminology derived from pathology.
> (1991: 17)

This inherent bias towards pathology is the main reason that we
find ourselves in a situation in which psychosomatic illness is so
much better understood than psychosomatic recovery and health.

Freud's suggestion that certain physical symptoms are an unconscious expression of psychological conflict (particularly, in Freud's
view, of sexual conflict) was revolutionary at the time it was made.
It came at the height of the 'laboratory period' of medicine, a
period characterised by research into the fine details of physiological mechanisms and a 'hard science' approach. To an even greater
extent than now, the human body was regarded by medical science
as an example of 'matter', devoid of meaning and unaffected by
emotional life.

In the early days, then, asserting the importance of psychological
factors in physical illness provoked intermittent clashes between
psychoanalysis on the one hand and science and medicine on the
other. This tension is not altogether resolved. Some physicians and
psychiatrists are still searching for the *presumed physiological basis* of
all illnesses, including mental illnesses. Others are more sympa-
thetic to the idea of a complex interplay of physiological, psychological and social factors. The Freudian idea that psychological
disturbance is on some occasions primary in the aetiology of physical symptoms has also become more widely accepted over time.

But to the extent that a peace has been agreed between medicine
and psychoanalysis, it is still a somewhat uneasy peace. The medical
tendency has been towards the delineation of a separate category of
'psychosomatic illnesses'. Psychoanalysts, on the other hand, have
been rather sceptical about the idea of a discrete and particular

group of psychosomatic illnesses. Franz Alexander (1950) argued that psychosomatic elements are common to *all* illnesses. Joyce McDougall (1974, 1989) came to a similar conclusion:

> The psychoanalyst finds himself constantly confronted with psychosomatic behaviour of a general kind in all of his analysands. (1974: 438)

There is a difference too between the 'official' medical line and the on-the-ground experience of the ordinary physician, who has ample opportunity to observe and reflect on the vicissitudes of health and their relationship to family difficulties, worries at work and so on. Brian Broom has described some of these experiences from the point of view of the physician in his excellent book *Somatic Illness and the Patient's Other Story* (Broom, 1997).

Psychoanalytic theory, particularly in its early formulations, reflected some of the assumptions of the dualistic paradigm (see also Chapter 4). In the same way that medicine had regarded the mental realm as unimportant, psychoanalysis has sometimes seemed to regard the physical realm as unworthy of detailed consideration. Action of any kind has been too readily identified with 'acting out'. The legitimate and indeed vital role of physical action in the management and expression of feelings has been underplayed.

In contrast to these tendencies within psychoanalytic theory, case studies have consistently pointed to the ongoing significance of the fact of embodiment, to the inseparable entanglement of physical and psychological facets of the self. Case studies have a special place in psychoanalysis. Verbatim extracts from the psychotherapy dialogue provide an experience-near basis for the formulation and ongoing re-evaluation of theory. Looking back over case studies spanning a period of many decades, we can see that the approach is essentially holistic, even where this has not been made explicit in the theoretical accounts. I can perhaps best illustrate the point with an extract from a case study written by Melanie Klein. It comes from her work with a child referred to as 'Fritz', who is relating a dream:

> The one chauffeur became sick, that was grandpapa. The other chauffeur said to him, 'You dirty beast, do you want your ears boxed, I will knock you down at once'. (I enquire who the other chauffeur was.) Me. And then our soldiers throw them all down – and smash the motor and

beat him and smear his face with coal and stuff coal in his mouth too... Then everyone was a soldier and I was the officer. I had a beautiful uniform and (he holds himself erect) I held myself like this, and then they all followed me. They took his gun away from him; he could only walk like this (here he doubles himself up). (Klein, 1921: 49)

Here Klein describes her client's bodily gestures as well as his words. It is clear that she is playing close attention to the finely coordinated operation of ideas, feelings, physical movements and gestures.

Recent years have been marked by changes in our perception of ourselves, as currents of thought opposed to the dualistic notion of separate-but-linked mind and body have gained ground. The influence of 'holistic' perspectives, where the human subject is seen as unitary – perceiving, thinking, feeling and always embodied – has become more telling. We increasingly understand ourselves as always 'embodied' on the one hand and as inevitably 'embedded' within a social and cultural context on the other. What I feel to be 'me' has a great deal to do with my experience of my physicality. At the same time, it is inseparable from the wider context that has shaped and continues to shape both my behaviour and my self-experience.

## Bringing meaning to experience

Psychoanalysis has had over 100 years of experience with the construction of personal narratives in a clinical setting. The starting point for a psychoanalytic dialogue is most often a certain kind of failure of self-understanding. The person seeking help cannot make sense of some aspect of his or her behaviour or experience.

Bion (1962) has eloquently described the process of 'containment', finding its original form in the maternal function of helping the infant to bring meaning to experience. Through her receptivity to the infant's experiences and her capacity to think about them, the mother makes bearable and mentally digestible events and experiences which the infant cannot manage alone. Eventually, the child is able to internalise this containing capacity. It forms the backbone of his adult ability to think about his experiences rather than to act impulsively or to express conflicts and difficulties through the development of psychological or physical symptoms. The role of the psychotherapist is also one of containment. He or she works to enable a client to find 'the words to say it' (Cardinal, 1993). A narrative is created which encompasses experiences that have hitherto been 'unstoried' and that are linked to dysfunction and distress.

Contemporary psychoanalytic perspectives fully acknowledge that an individual's social and cultural context colours his or her self-narrative. Nevertheless, psychoanalysts believe on the whole that this narrative remains a personal creation. What we witness is an *intertwining* of the cultural and the personal. This is not to deny that cultural norms and environmental conditions map out a certain range of possibilities. We are aware that even the experiences we feel to be most personal and non-negotiable – for example, what it is to have a satisfactory sexual experience, or to be a good mother – are culturally shaped and vary from one time and place to another. Nevertheless, within this culturally delimited range, we believe that an individual is involved in the task of bringing his or her own individual meaning to experience. He or she is constantly active, whether consciously or unconsciously, in his or her particular interpretation of and response to a particular environment. It is this *individual meaning-making endeavour* that is highlighted in a psychoanalytic approach.

## Winnicott and 'indwelling'

> It is really much easier, and more usual, for a doctor to write about illness. Through the study of illness we come to the study of much that is important about health. But the doctor's assumption that health is a relative absence of disease is not good enough. The word health has its own meaning in a positive way, so that absence of disease is no more than the starting point for healthy life. (Winnicott, 1988: 1)

D.W. Winnicott was unusual in developing a specific psychoanalytic focus on health in the positive sense. His starting point for thinking about health was the notion of 'the psyche indwelling in the soma':

> The infant becomes a person, an individual in his own right. Associated with this attainment is the infant's psychosomatic existence, which begins to take on a personal pattern; I have referred to this as the psyche indwelling in the soma. (Winnicott, 1960b: 45)

As described earlier, Winnicott saw the achievement of 'psycho-somatic existence' with a 'personal pattern' as deriving initially from the mother's ability to join up physiological and psychological aspects of her experience – during pregnancy, the birth process and feeding and caring for her baby. Later experiences such as crawling, learning to walk and perhaps eventually climbing mountains or playing a sport continue this joining up process.

Winnicott repeatedly returns to the physical dimension of living, which for him is absolutely entangled with mental and spiritual aspects of experience. The idea of 'the psyche indwelling in the soma' is explored in its own right in several of Winnicott's key papers. In addition, it is woven through other, better known, aspects of his writing, for example his work on 'holding' and 'handling' in infancy and his exploration of the value of play. It is central to his concept of 'true self', described by Winnicott (1960a) himself as 'little more that the summation of sensory-motor aliveness'.

From this simple sense of 'aliveness' emanates the spontaneous gesture of the newborn infant. It may be something as simple as a certain way of kicking or of beginning a feed. If the gesture is received and responded to, the foundation is laid for the development of what Bollas (1993) calls the individual's 'personal idiom'. Over time, the idea takes shape in Winnicott's work that a sense of being self-centred in the body is an essential precondition for healthy and enjoyable living.

A 'false self' (1960a) is also identified by Winnicott as an essential part of the adult repertoire. Like all psychoanalysts, Winnicott is deeply involved in the consideration of a person's capacity to relate to others, and a capacity for relationship is seen as fundamental to health. The false self functions both to protect the essentially private germ of the 'true self' from exposure and to oil the wheels of useful social interactions. In health, though, there is a point beyond which compromise feels intolerable and is resisted.

Whether he is considering the question of play, of mothering or of personal authenticity, Winnicott's writing returns to a discussion of the internal and external factors that support or obstruct an individual's capacity for relationship. He sees a feeling of being connected to, grounded in, one's own physicality as crucially important. It is synonymous with access to the 'true self' elements which enable an individual to feel uniquely like himself or herself.

It is the basis for a 'gut feeling', without which the individual has no internally experienced basis for his or her actions or plans. The term 'indwelling' refers to this feeling of 'at-oneness' with one's own physicality. For Winnicott, health involves these two inseparable aspects of being – a potential for authentic relationships with others and a firm grounding within one's own physicality.

As I have taken the idea of psychosomatic indwelling as a central theme, I shall digress from this discussion to present a picture of what a good quality of 'indwelling' might look like.

## Sylvia's dream

This dream narrative, recounted by a client, is reproduced here with her permission.

I dream of my son John, who is twenty and living away from home. In the dream, he has won an award for his university project and I am invited along to see the project performed. I am shown to a door off a corridor. I walk through and find myself in a large hall, which John has planted with a great mass of tall weeds. The artistic 'happening' that follows involves these weeds being mown down from one edge of the hall and scythed down from the other. While this goes on, John sits with his legs draped languorously over the arm of his chair.

As the mower and the scythe meet and I think that matters are drawing to a close, John slips off. I am a bit taken aback and wonder where he has gone. A few minutes later, he reappears in the doorway, dressed in a white T-shirt and shiny red shorts and with a white football held aloft in both hands. He gives a loud whoop and rushes in, followed by half a dozen of his friends. They fill the hall and play a wild and hilarious game of football on the felled weeds.

When I wake up, I feel John's presence still in the room. This is so absolutely like him – his quirky originality, his sense of fun, – and those sudden shifts from being really languid to buzzing with energy.

The dreamer reflects that her son's physical self-expression, his whole way of inhabiting his body, carries and communicates the essence of who he is and how he is. The dream and the dreamer's reflections convey the essential idea that physical self-experience and self-expression are both *meaningful* and *communicative*. These are the ideas inherent in Winnicott's concept of the 'psyche indwelling in the soma'.

Within psychoanalysis, Winnicott's distinctive emphasis on physicality characterises his work. While sharing traditional psychoanalytic concerns – with the human activity of 'meaning-making', with the influence of the past and of the envisaged future on experience in the present, with the influence of unconscious factors on our perceptions and our behaviour – Winnicott reserves a particular place for our experience of embodiment:

> Winnicott put at the centre of his developmental model not a mythic conflict between incompatible forces but 'the localisation of self in one's body'. (Phillips, 1988: 78)

## The centrality of narrative

Narrative theory shares certain features with postmodernism and social constructionism, to which I shall turn my (not particularly expert) attention in the next chapter. However, narrative theory leaves more space than social constructionism for the influence of the particular make-up of a particular individual. Personal characteristics, some of them inborn, are recognised as playing a role both in the eliciting of experiences and in the interpretation of experiences that come along:

> Different people tend to construct experiences of the same event differently, each for reasons of his or her own. Many of these reasons originate early in life and therefore give rise to primitive forms of emotional and cognitive experience that persist unconsciously and influentially into adult life.
>
> These individual variations add individual coloring to otherwise standardized responses to the conventions of one's culture. (Schafer, 1992: xiv)

From a narrative point of view, perception itself involves interpretation, and it is normal to re-interpret events as time moves on, as the context within which they are embedded changes. We can identify many examples of such re-interpretation in everyday living:

At the end of a tournament, top Swiss tennis player Marc Rosset experienced a delay in getting to the airport, that caused him to miss his plane. He felt considerably inconvenienced and frustrated at the time. But the plane he should have been on crashed, with numerous fatalities. Later, Rosset appeared on television voicing his relief and gratitude alongside feelings of confusion and disbelief.

When events transpire which cause such a dramatic shift in interpretation, the experience can be quite disorienting. In the normal course of events, re-interpretations of events tend to come about more gradually. Sometimes, we may 'catch' ourselves stating or acting on a long-held belief out of habit. In the same moment, we may understand that the belief no longer holds true for us. In the world of interpretation and re-interpretation, there is no final closure: there is always room for another 'version':

> We continually reconstruct the way we understand ourselves. This is what clients seek to do in therapy, hence the need to talk, to tell one's story. (Howe, 1993: 137)

Some psychoanalytic writers (and a much larger number of systemic family therapists) put the 'storying' aspect of psychotherapy at the very centre of their project. For example, Rose and Loewenthal (1998), discussing the need for a counselling/psychotherapy service for people with a cleft lip, explicitly adopt this position:

> This study will focus on the 'talking' aspect of therapy, as opposed to which theoretical framework should be employed, and as such endorses the view that the simple act of giving voice to one's worries and concerns is itself therapeutic. (Rose and Lowenthal, 1998: 106)

The Australian family therapists White and Epson (1990) emphasise that material emerging in psychotherapy is not a pre-formed story which is then narrated, but rather the product of the creative act of 'storying'. The story does not exist prior to being recounted. It is created in the context of its telling. That which remains 'unstoried' is in a sense an inchoate mass. This account draws strength from sources outside the psychotherapy setting. The famous British actress Fiona Shaw became mentally ill following the birth of her second child and 'storied' this experience. This is what she said about the process of writing the book:

When I began writing this book, I did so in the effort to shore myself up against the whirling chaos of my mind. I was in fear of disintegration, though I couldn't, and still can't, describe what I mean by that... What has been important has been the act of turning blankness and confusion into narrative coherence, however provisional. (1998: 2)

Individual studies of psychotherapy outcomes can demonstrate the usefulness of one particular approach. But, somewhat to the chagrin of practitioners who wish to claim the exclusive efficacy of their own style of work, broad overviews of psychotherapy outcome studies have consistently failed to identify any one form of counselling or psychotherapy as being consistently more helpful than any other. The indirect implication of these outcome studies is perhaps that a skilful management of the elements common to *all* psychotherapeutic approaches – narration and relationship – is the key factor in a good psychotherapy outcome. According to the evidence so far, specific techniques, which differ between different therapeutic approaches, are of only secondary importance.

Corroborating evidence for this proposition has emerged from an unexpected source. Subjects taking part in research that took the 'biographical research' form of long and loosely structured interviews spontaneously described an improvement in well-being as a consequence of their participation (personal communication, Susannah Rupp, 1998). The interviewers were not psychotherapists, and the improvement in well-being had not been predicted. Nevertheless, the key elements of narration, attentive listening and dialogue were all in place and seem to have had an unintended therapeutic effect.

## Surfaces and inner spaces

A complication that cannot be avoided when writing about health and physicality is the dual meaning of the word 'body'. On the one hand, the body is an object in external space and can be perceived as such by ourselves and by others. On the other hand, it is the locus of our 'indwelling'; it is what I think of as 'me':

Reality begins with the body, which gives us a shape, existence and
boundaries. It is the carrier of our being in the world, the *sine qua non*
of living on the earth. (Blackmer Dexter, 1989: 28)

It is with our subjective experiences, rather than with our behaviour as perceived from the outside, that psychoanalysis has always
been most concerned. In the area of physicality, our subjective
sense of ourselves as 'embodied' or 'indwelling' emerges from
many interrelated experiences. Winnicott describes how the
handling we receive as babies gives us a sense of a personal shape
and of physical boundaries.

Jungian psychology has enjoyed a close association with art
therapy, dance and theatre. As a consequence of their involvement
with creative uses of movement activities, certain Jungian
psychotherapists have become particularly sensitive to the psychological importance of movement and of proprioceptive function,
and this is reflected in their clinical work and their writing (see, for
example, Payne, 1992).

The sense of proprioception – sometimes called the 'kines-
thetic' or 'positional' sense – is brought into play at the beginning
of life as a consequence of handling experiences and of our own
self-initiated movements. Through proprioception, we know the
position and speed of movement of different parts of our body
without the need for visual feedback. It is because of my proprioceptive capacities that I may be able to perform a forward roll with
my eyes closed (although perhaps not such a neat one as when I
was younger!). Through our proprioceptive capacities, we have a
sense of our bodies from the inside, and Joan Blackmer Dexter
(cited above) has in fact referred to proprioception as a kind of
'inner touching'.

Paradoxically, the importance of proprioception becomes more
evident if it becomes damaged. While it is impaired, we are help-
less in many ways and tend to lose a sense of properly inhabiting
our bodies.

A colleague was approached for psychotherapy by a man who had
contracted a virus after he cut his finger. He had suffered damage to his
nervous system which had disabled his proprioceptive faculties. He could not
stand up or sit down except by closely observing the movements of his limbs
and relying upon visual feedback. Thus he knew he had moved his leg

because he had seen it move. On several occasions when he tried to turn over in bed, the man accidentally flung himself on to the floor. In the dark and without proprioceptive feedback with regard to position or speed of his limbs, he could not apply the right amount of pressure to complete the movement safely. While this situation continued, psychological disorientation involving a 'not-me' sense of the body was a key aspect of this unfortunate man's distress.

The body as object, perceived by others and by ourselves as if from an external point of view, is also an aspect of our being. Self-esteem is in part a function of how we imagine we are seen. Sometimes our self-perceptions can become very distorted, as when an anorexic young woman sees herself as 'fat'. Health requires the maintenance of a delicate balance between our experience of the body we see (or think we see) reflected in the mirror and the body experienced from within.

As well as bestowing the mixed blessing of a sedentary lifestyle (of which more in Chapter 11), contemporary society places a marked emphasis on appearances, on the surfaces of things including the surfaces of our bodies. Whether it is to be perfected, sculpted, deprived, obsessed over, injured, ignored, neglected or narcissistically worshipped, the body tends increasingly to be regarded as *other than* the self. Attention is lavished on physical appearance while physicality as experienced from within fades from consciousness. Although the body is clearly both a palpable and a visible object existing in external space, *and* the home of our being experienced from within, the latter cognisance seems fragile and tends to slip away.

When the body as object is a dominant cultural theme, it is perhaps not surprising that a sense of indwelling can prove difficult to maintain. In this situation, we might expect to see an increased incidence of certain kinds of problem, which fundamentally involve a dissociation between the mental and physical aspects of the self. I believe that this is what we are in fact witnessing in our increasingly numerous encounters with psychosomatic disturbances. Such disturbances find many forms of expression, for example in unexplained physical symptoms, in eating disorders and in incidents of self-harm. At the other end of the scale is the positive enjoyment of health, which involves a sense of wholeness and of being grounded in one's own physicality.

In considering the continuum of possibilities, a number of questions come to mind. How does what Winnicott calls a 'good quality of indwelling' come into being (or fail to come into being) in infancy? How can the enjoyment of health be supported and safeguarded? How can we work effectively with psychosomatic difficulties in adult life? These are the questions that will be addressed in Parts II and III of the book through the exploration of individual body storylines.

# CHAPTER 3

# Thinking about Health

(I refer to)... the inherited tendency of each individual to achieve a unity of psyche and soma, and experiential identity of the spirit or psyche and the totality of physical functioning. (Winnicott, 1966: 112)

*Is health the absence of physical illness or is it more, or less, than that? And is it really useful to separate out 'mental' and 'physical' health? This chapter considers a number of different approaches to 'holistic' health. Characteristic features of the holistic perspectives on health offered by phenomenology, humanistic psychotherapy and Eastern philosophical frameworks are described and considered in terms of their relationship to the theme of somatic awareness and to psychoanalytic understandings.*

## Psychosomatic illness and psychosomatic health

Lisa is sitting in the chair opposite, telling me again about the pain in her left side, a kind of recurrent 'stitch' that sometimes spreads around into her lower back.

*Lisa:* The physiotherapist only saw me for six weeks. She said that, to be quite honest, she couldn't find anything wrong. But the pain is still there. I went back to my GP and she said she thinks it must be psychosomatic. (Lisa shoots me a piercing look.) Is that what you think?

*Maggie:* (pauses to think) ...I think you're asking me whether I think you bring the pain upon yourself. Is that right?

The word 'psychosomatic', not infrequently introduced by a client into a session, is no easier to pin down than the word 'health'. For many people, there is a definite stigma attached to it.

And it is true, unfortunately, that the term is still sometimes used to imply that a person is not 'really' ill at all, in short that he or she is malingering. It is important to emphasise that psychosomatic illnesses, if indeed they exist as a separate category, are as 'real' as any other illnesses. From the onset of the difficulties, the suffering is real, the symptoms are real. The initial stages of the illness involve a disturbance of function without any evident organ damage, but there is ample evidence that organ damage can follow, sometimes with life-threatening consequences.

The physician George Groddeck (1866–1934), one of Freud's early colleagues, strongly asserted that there is no basic difference between organic and mental illness (Groddeck, 1977). I find myself in broad agreement with his conclusion. Fascinating as it is, I shall not attempt to review the psychoanalytic literature on psychosomatic illness here; to do so would be to stray too far from my task of writing a book with a central focus on health, recovery and everyday living. Fortunately, there are excellent accounts of psychosomatic pathology already available, for example in the work of Alexander (1950), Wilson and Mintz (1989) and McDougall (1974, 1989).

The *Concise Oxford English Dictionary* (1995) offers two definitions of the word 'psychosomatic':

> (of an illness etc.) caused or aggravated by mental conflict, stress, etc.;
>
> of the mind and body together.

The first definition is dated later than the first; it is the current medical definition. Unfortunately, it is sometimes taken to imply that the sufferer is in some way to blame for his or her illness. This is not a necessary implication, for surely no shame should attach to an illness to which one has been predisposed by difficult or overwhelming life circumstances? In contemporary Western culture, though, we are supposed to be in full control of our circumstances and of their effects upon us. To have succumbed to 'mental conflict' and 'stress' and to have allowed it to make us ill is apparently reprehensible. The sense of shame that some people feel when their illness is described as 'psychosomatic' is a major psychological problem in itself. At times, it fuels a truly desperate quest for a physical explanation for symptoms, which in turn translates into a never-ending succession of expensive and unpleasant medical investigations (see Broom, 1997).

The main problem seems to lie in the use of the phrase 'caused by', for almost everybody seems able to accept that illnesses are 'aggravated' by mental conflict and stress. Even something as simple as a toothache seems to be aggravated by loneliness or over-work, although it seems unlikely to have been 'caused' by these phenomena. With regard to causation, we do well to acknowledge what Bion called a 'cloud of unknowing'. Some symptoms are not associated with a particular disease, while there are some diseases that have no particular symptoms. Sometimes it is only when we find out more that we become aware of having been in ignorance. The illness porphyria, long thought of as a mental illness and dramatised in the film *The Madness of King George*, was eventually discovered to be the result of a specific genetic disorder involving the abnormal metabolism of porphyrin pigments and their excretion in the urine.

In any event, linear cause and effect explanations are fast falling from favour. What we have in their place are feedback loops, field theories, chaos theories, models of causation which, in common with psychoanalytic theory, suggest that events are multiply determined and that causative factors interact in a complex and somewhat unpredictable manner. And as psychological factors emerge more and more clearly as playing a role in all of our major contemporary illnesses, there is no real case for singling out a certain subset of illnesses and asserting that they and they alone are 'caused' by unwelcome (yet frequently unavoidable) psychological phenomena. To consider the *meaning* that the client finds in his or her illness is one thing; to speak in terms of cause and effect is quite another.

In considering matters of health, recovery and everyday living, it is clear that the first definition of 'psychosomatic' offered above will not take us far. It applies exclusively to illness. We need then to turn to the second definition: 'of mind and body together'. This definition poses a certain kind of challenge, for it can be argued that every human experience, every human action, is of mind and body together, has both a psychological and a physiological reality. These realities stand as different and equally valid 'versions' or descriptions of the same event. Neither can be reduced to the other. From a psychological point of view, formulating and writing this sentence is a meaningful unit of human experience. From a physiological point of view, it can be described in terms of a complex interplay of electrical and chemical currents within my central nervous system and my arm and finger muscles. What is true of writing a sentence is true, I believe, of all human experiences. If we agree to use the word 'psychosomatic' in this very general way, we must take on board the idea that human experience is a ubiquitous psychosomatic soup in which we swim. Within this soup, it is still possible to pick out specific ingredients for detailed study. Later in this book, for example, I pick out experiences of movement and touch for detailed study in terms of their contribution to a robust and alive sense of psychosomatic indwelling.

Psychosomatic health finds expression in a harmony of verbal self-expression and body language. The body and the word act in concert. This is evident to the onlooker as all aspects of our self-expression convey the same message and the same feeling. And in subjective terms, we have the experience of 'firing on all cylinders'. In the following extract from a piece of counselling work, a client moves closer towards this state of psychosomatic health as the session progresses.

Susan, who has decided to leave London to take up a very good job offer, comes to a therapy session and begins by telling me that a buyer has been found for her flat and that she is 'really pleased'. The note of cheerfulness in her voice is strained and her shoulders have a definite slump to them. I feel a kind of tightening around my heart. There is a conspicuous contrast between what is said and what is communicated in a bodily way. I say, 'You're happy that your plans to leave are moving forward?' I try to maintain a neutral tone but I know my voice expresses a certain reluctance to accept the statement at face value. We sit and think for a while.

After a few minutes, Susan begins to cry. She tells me she is afraid of leaving London, where she grew up and where she feels at home. She tells me how much she will miss me and the particular kind of space in her life that the psychotherapy sessions provide. Her words and her body language are once more in accord.

Although Susan is more overtly unhappy at the end of the session than when she entered the room, her quality of indwelling/psychosomatic health has improved. Susan is now in touch with her visceral self; she is functioning as a whole. Like

Winnicott, I believe that a 'good enough' quality of indwelling is a necessary condition for the full recovery of health in its wider sense. Before we can find our way forward, we must have a proper sense of where we are and how we are in the here and now.

In view of the vagaries of individual interpretation, and thus of each individual's understanding of what it means to be 'healthy', it may seem foolhardy to venture any general thoughts on the subject. Nevertheless, I shall try to summarise some of the positive elements I believe to be involved in psychosomatic health, in the hope that others will discuss and add to the list. I would include an overall sense of well-being, the possibility of spontaneity and creativity, and a capacity for recovery from physical and psychological blows. I would also include an acceptance of our changing physical state, including variations in our experience of wellness and illness. And, because an individual is not an isolated phenomenon, I would consider it essential to refer to the ability to enter into authentic relationships with others. The experience of a certain level of energy or vitality seems important too. Phenomenological psychoanalyst John Heaton refers to being 'in touch with the vitality of living which has no end in itself' (Heaton, 1998). These, then, are some of the elements I have in mind when I use the phrase 'psychosomatic health'.

## The enigma of health: contributions from phenomenology

Phenomenology takes as its remit the description and in-depth examination of phenomena as they appear in the everyday world. The central concept of 'being-in-the-world', introduced by Heidegger (1927), emphasises that we have no 'free-standing' existence: our experiences, thoughts and actions are constantly and inevitably embedded in a context.

Although dualism has remained in the ascendant in Western philosophy, the alternative strand of thinking represented by phenomenology has continued to develop. Merleau-Ponty (1962), Boss (1963) and many other phenomenologists have argued against a Cartesian framework for philosophy and science, against the reductionism of the scientific method and against attempts to divide the human subject into a body and a mind:

My existence as subjectivity is merely one with my existence as a body
and with the existence of the world. (Merleau-Ponty, 1962: 408)

John Heaton is a contemporary psychoanalyst strongly influenced by phenomenology who has pointed to the absurdity of a
dualistic conception of the human subject:

> In our everyday activities we do not experience our minds and bodies
> as being distinct separate things. When we sneeze or we laugh we do
> not say 'my body sneezes' or 'my mind laughs'. Such language sounds
> false and artificial. (Heaton, 1967: 216)

Heaton goes on to argue that it is our ever-present awareness of
embodiment that gives us a sense of self and of an external world:

> It is only because we are embodied selves that we can apprehend
> external objects at all for the fact of embodiment makes it necessary for
> us to observe objects from a place and it is this which gives them their
> objectivity. (1967: 217)

Phenomenology, ahead of postmodernism, has opposed the
building of overarching, 'totalising' (Levinas, 1978) theories, which
claim to encompass all events and to hold true in all situations. In
place of the scientific method, with its ultimate aim of total control
and predictability, there is an emphasis on description and reflection. Phenomenology states that we are all subject to certain
'givens' of existence – that we will at some point die, that we are
essentially alone, that we cannot know what the future will hold.
Within the context of these 'givens' and in spite of the vicissitudes
of fate, we are responsible for bringing meaning to our lives, both
through the interpretation and re-interpretation of our experiences and through our actions in relation to them. (For an accessible account of these ideas in a psychotherapy context, see *The
Interpreted World* by Ernesto Spinelli, 1989.)

The phenomenological emphasis on observation and description, and the antipathy shown towards 'totalising' theories, which
tend to rigidify into unquestioned dogma, accords well with Winnicott's approach to the human subject. Winnicott shared with
phenomenologists several areas of core concern, including the
issues of embodiment and personal authenticity. However, he was

less interested in these issues in the abstract than in the struggles of *individual* infants, children and adults. A phenomenological approach with a focus on the individual is also a characteristic of psychoanalytic infant observation, in which the primary emphasis is on observation and description. Discussion in terms of theoretical concepts comes into the picture at a later stage.

Phenomenologists have been at the forefront of the interrogation of the idea of health. They have engaged with the question: what do we mean when we use the words 'health' or 'healthy?' They argue that health is best understood in terms of an *affirmation of potential*, rather than in terms of a fixed biomedical or even a biopsychosocial construct (see Fox, 1999). This point of view has an important bearing on the issues raised in Chapter 1, where I raised the issue of the myth of perfect health. The idea that we should be constantly well, or else be able to identify something specific that has gone wrong, is closely allied to the denial of mortality that we encounter in a number of different contexts.

A counsellor brought to supervision a client whose 87-year-old father was suffering from cancer. The client wanted to know what had caused her father to get cancer. Was it her mother's coldness towards him, the way she grumbled about him getting under her feet in the years following his retirement? It took some time to bring to light the question behind the question, namely 'Why does my father have to die?'

Heaton has commented explicitly on the elusive quality of the concept of health. Health, he suggests, is hard to pin down. It is not an absolute but rather something we move towards and slip away from:

> Now health is enigmatic. Illness is something we know quite a lot about whereas health is more mysterious. (Heaton, 1998: 38)

Rather than being something fixed and static, health is a matter of a tendency, *a reaching for* or *a movement towards* a state of well-being, most recognisable in our resilience, in our ability to bounce back, in our tendency towards recovery. In this sense, health is 'dynamic', defined in the *Concise Oxford English Dictionary* (1995) as 'energetic; active; potent'.

# Postmodernism, social constructionism and health

A great deal of writing emanating from a postmodern perspective has emerged over the past few decades. In addition, many books have been written on the subject of postmodernism itself. Here, I offer a simplified summary of some key points and consider their implications for thinking about health:

> Postmodernism is a rejection of both the idea that there can be an ultimate truth and of structuralism, the idea that the world as we see it is the result of hidden structures. (Burr, 1995: 13)

Postmodern thinking evolved primarily within the fields of literary criticism, cultural studies, art and architecture. It offers a broad intellectual framework that stands in contrast to 'modernism', the intellectual movement which preceded it. Postmodernism rejects the assumption, characteristic of modernism and of scientific enquiry, that the nature of reality can be discovered and pinned down through the application of reason and rationality. It has argued persuasively, and with reference to many different examples, that what is regarded as 'true', 'real' and 'normal' changes over time and varies considerably between one culture and another.

Vivien Burr (cited above) comments that the terms 'postmodernism' and 'poststructuralism' are often used interchangeably. Marxism, which explains social phenomena in terms of the underlying economic structures, and Freudian theory, which offers an account of psychological phenomena in terms of underlying psychic structures, are often cited as examples of 'structuralist' theories. Such theories are incompatible with a postmodern framework, where the idea of underlying structure is explicitly rejected. The quest for universal rules and structures, particularly in relation to human behaviour, is seen as both misguided and disrespectful of cultural difference. Postmodernism advocates instead the description of a multiplicity of coexisting and situation-dependent realities.

The term 'social constructionism', broadly speaking, refers to the expression and development of postmodern themes in the field of the social sciences. In relation to psychoanalysis, a key feature of social constructionism is the rejection of 'grand theories' or 'metanarratives', such as those set out by early psychoanalytic theorists. Such metanarratives fail to meet the criteria of social constructionism on account of their explicit or implicit claims to universal applicability.

In its pure form, social constructionism rejects absolutely the idea of an inborn kernel of individuality that shapes the way in which a person responds to his or her environment. The rejection of the possibility that a human being brings something of his own to the party when he or she arrives in the world stands in stark contrast to even the most 'environmental' versions of psychoanalytic theory. In terms of other psychological theories, such a position is perhaps compatible only with the more extreme forms of behaviourism, in which an individual is regarded at birth as a 'blank slate' to be written upon by experience.

It can be argued that even Lacanian theory, which has aligned itself explicitly with postmodern thinking, fails fully to meet the criteria of social constructionism. Lacan proposes a 'gap' or a 'lack' at the centre of being as the universal endowment of every individual. This 'lack' is described by Lacan as deriving from the biological prematurity of the infant at birth. But can this lack be properly thought of as 'nothing' when Lacan attributes to it a powerful energetic quality, which sets in motion a quest for true recognition – the desire for the desire of the other? And is there not a claim to universal applicability implicit in this idea of a basic lack at the centre of human experience?

In spite of these complications, psychoanalysis shares certain important affinities with social constructionism. Both have been involved in challenging scientific claims of objectivity and have argued that observation is always affected by the person doing the observing. Both emphasise the interpreted nature of experience and caution against the assumption that things are as they appear. Both implicitly advocate 'a critical stance towards taken-for-granted knowledge' (Burr, 1995).

Postmodern thinking overlaps with and builds on the phenomenological viewpoint outlined above. One of the primary themes of postmodernism, the shifting, socially constructed and constantly re-narrated nature of experience, is repeatedly referred to in this book. In the light of the understanding that all knowledge is both local and provisional, I acknowledge that the conception of health arrived at and fleshed out here is unlikely to be meaningful in all places and at all times. For people who reside outside a Western cultural context, the perspective offered may have little or no relevance.

The French philosopher Michel Foucault has developed postmodern dicourse in a particular direction through an in-depth analysis of the relationship between information and power. He argues that the individual's knowledge that information about him is held by the state, combined with the individual's ignorance of exactly what is and is not known, constitutes a powerful form of social and political control (Foucault, 1984). In contemporary Western society, this invisible form of social control has largely replaced control through physical restraint.

Where health and illness are concerned, the question of access to information has a clear and practical importance. Up until recently, only the physician had access to the relevant information, in the form of the patient's medical records and case notes, and the relevant expertise. This situation placed the patient in a powerless position, exacerbated by his or her understanding that the physician held relevant information, without knowing what that information was or whether or not it would be disclosed on request. The medical profession's exclusivity of knowledge brought with it the power not only to determine the treatments we receive if we become ill, but also to control the parameters within which we think about health and illness. Through the deconstruction of medical expertise, postmodern discourse has begun to challenge this hegemony of the medical expert. Calls for the demystification of medicine, our increased determination to be involved in decisions relating to medical interventions, the hard-won right of access to our own medical records and our enthusiasm for self-selected treatments and complementary therapies are all examples of a *Zeitgeist* in tune with postmodern thinking.

These changes have also been pushed forward by the rapidly expanding availability on the Internet of complex and specialised information on just about every disease known to medical science. Increasingly, the patient is in a position to gain access to relevant research and information and thus to discuss his or her health problem with the 'expert' on more equal terms. It is still the case, of course, that physicians control access to treatment resources. I have recently learned of a situation in which a patient felt it imperative to 'dumb down' her extensive knowledge of her medical condition so as not to displease the expert and run the risk, fantasised or otherwise, of being moved down the waiting list.

Such limitations notwithstanding, information empowers us to make appropriate decisions and plans. Where relevant information is unavailable, odd situations tend to evolve. Some individuals who discovered themselves to be HIV positive at the beginning of the AIDS epidemic thought that they only had a few more years of life left to them, this being the best available information at the time. Some of them sold up their property and spent their money in the interests of immediate enjoyment, only to find later that they had an (unknown) number of years ahead of them and rather little left in the way of material resources.

In contrast, the writer Edward Said was able to learn, before the onset of any symptoms, that he was suffering from the illness 'CLL' – chronic lymphocytic leukaemia. Said's knowledge of his condition emerged from a routine blood test combined with his insistence on acquiring as much information as was available at the earliest possible moment. The information had no effect on the trajectory of the disease. Nevertheless, the understanding that his life 'would be shorter and more difficult now' led Said to undertake emotionally important and long-deferred visits to Palestine and to Cairo and to begin writing his memoir (Said, 1999).

A further characteristic of postmodern thinking is a shift of emphasis away from antecedent causes and on to future-oriented questions (see, for example, Elliott and Frosh, 1995). With reference to health, we may ask: 'Does this particular symptom have a purpose? What is being communicated and to what end? What is this health-enhancing practice *for* and where is it leading? A future-oriented stance provides a useful corrective to the over-application in both medicine and psychoanalysis of traditional cause and effect-type explanations, which deny the anticipated future its proper role in the shaping of the present.

## Humanistic psychotherapy approaches

We know that, for most people, the first idea that comes to mind when thinking about health is the idea of being free from illness. Health, in this sense, is about what is absent (illness) rather than about what is present. Although it is commonplace, this way of thinking seems rather unsatisfactory. Should it not be possible to articulate what we mean by health in a *positive* sense? Humanistic psychotherapy and the 'growth movement' arose in part as a corrective to the psychoanalytic overemphasis on pathology. The humanistic concern with health as a positive is entirely valid and has important precedents. For example, in trying to move towards a more positive conception of health, the World Health Organization (WHO) defined it in 1948 as:

> A state of complete physical, mental, and social well-being and... not merely the absence of disease or infirmity. (cited in Sheridan and Radmacher, 1992)

In some cases, the perspective on health embraced by humanistic psychotherapies has the same rather Utopian flavour as the WHO definition cited above. 'A state of complete physical, mental and social well-being' is a tall order, and there is a risk here of promulgating the 'myth of perfect health' referred to in Chapter 1. Of course, we do experience such a state. It is perhaps present in the moments described by humanist psychotherapist Abraham Maslow as 'peak experiences', and we value these highly. At the same time, it needs to be recognised that such moments are rare and special, and are likely to remain so. They are not the usual stuff of everyday living.

Bodywork psychotherapies come under the broad umbrella of humanistic approaches. However, they have distinctive features of their own, and in some quarters a fruitful dialogue exists between psychoanalytic and bodywork approaches. Some of the areas of agreement and of difference are considered later in the book (see Chapters 4 and 8).

## Eastern philosophical approaches

The psychoanalytic account presented in this book has areas of overlap with Eastern philosophical frameworks. I am aware that many readers will be familiar with the association between Eastern philosophies and the idea of the unity of mind, body and spirit. Medical practices deriving from Eastern philosophies generally make no formal distinction between mental and physical illness. In Chinese medicine, for example, all symptoms, whatever their nature, are seen as a disturbance of balance between the different elements enjoined within the individual.

Eastern philosophies have become more familiar in contemporary Western society as the many therapies and health practices based in them have risen in popularity. Such therapies and practices include acupuncture, shiatsu, Ayurvedic medicine, Reiki, yoga and meditation. Most of them have a very long history in their country of origin. The success enjoyed by 'alternative' and 'complementary' practitioners (who are probably well used by the sections of the population likely to be reading this book) reflects our current disenchantment with the biomedical model of health and the practices that derive from it. I do not claim a deep knowledge of the subject of Eastern philosophies, and it is on the basis of a limited understanding that I offer some comments on the perspectives offered by such philosophies on the subject of health.

Health practices based in Eastern philosophies are, for the most part, essentially holistic. In contrast to traditional Western medicine, they centre on health as a positive rather than on illness or the absence of illness. Health is usually conceptualised as a state of *balance* between different elements or energies. Illness, whether of the kind we would normally label 'physical' or 'mental', involves a disturbance of such balance. Treatment aims to support a person's own natural tendency to restore balance and harmony, and thus to regain good health. Practitioners whose approach is centred in Eastern philosophy will seek to work with the whole person, often asking for a detailed personal history as well as a description of troubling physical symptoms. Unlike the Western philosophy of phenomenology, described above, Eastern philosophies have a long history of underpinning health practices.

Health care approaches based on Eastern philosophical principles clearly have a great deal to offer, but there are certain difficulties inherent in the transfer of Eastern sets of beliefs and values onto Western soil. For example, as I understand it, the idea of Karma involves the belief that we are directly or indirectly responsible for all events that befall us. Negative experiences and suffering are seen as the consequence of negative actions, whether undertaken in this life or in a past life. This belief system is at odds with the beliefs, be they religious or secular, of most people living in the Western world. In the form in which it has arrived within our culture, the philosophy of Karma seems to 'blame the victim' to an unacceptable degree.

Where a therapy involves only a 'hands-on' treatment, such considerations are unlikely to give rise to problems. Where experience needs to be narrated and discussed, however, a 'home-grown' approach has advantages. Eastern philosophies, with their very different cultural and religious roots, do not offer a familiar and accessible language and are not necessarily well suited to understanding the difficulties in living that are shaped by the context of contemporary Western society.

Complementary therapies often involve specific experiences of touch and/or movement as part of an endeavour to enhance somatic awareness and to bring different aspects of the individual into balance. I have found such therapies to be of great benefit, both to myself and to a number of clients. This benefit can be amplified when a client works through his or her experience of such therapies in a psychoanalytic setting. An excellent opportunity arises for the integration into the body storyline of emotional and bodily sensations experienced during the course of the physical therapy.

## Somatic awareness

It is probably stating the obvious to say that many of the clients who come for psychotherapy of any kind suffer from an impoverishment of somatic awareness. The client's poor access to 'gut feelings' is often very striking. The body may be referred to as if it were a 'not me' appendage. Lisa, talking about her inexplicable symptoms, said to me: 'My body plays tricks on me.' Clients sometimes refer explicitly to a *lack of body sensation* that borders on numbness and is itself a cause of psychological pain.

A meeting point between humanistic psychotherapy approaches, practices based in Eastern philosophy, health psychology (described in the next chapter) and psychoanalytic approaches lies in their common endeavour to bring about an increase in what is often referred to as 'somatic awareness'. The terms 'somatic awareness' and 'psychosomatic indwelling' both refer to the sense of knowing one's state of being from within. Different healing approaches take different routes in an endeavour to enable the restoration and/or enhancement of somatic awareness.

The approaches to healing described in this chapter address issues of somatic awareness by encouraging, and often teaching, the client to do something new, to engage in an activity which is not a part of his or her normal repertoire. The range of activities involved is enormous, ranging from a bioenergetics exercise or a group exercise involving movement and physical contact, to chanting and meditation. In each case, the participant begins by doing something new and unusual. Sometimes, the practitioner also does something to the client, for example gives a massage.

It is probably clear by now that I do not question the psychological value of physical activities. On the contrary, I believe that it is only through the use of our bodies, through our engagement with touch and movement activities, that we can hope to achieve and maintain a good level of somatic awareness. At the same time, we need to understand that *many clients have unconsciously and necessarily reduced their level of somatic awareness as a survival strategy*, as a way of defending against unbearable psychological pain. For these clients, engaging in a new physical activity under the direction of a third party carries certain risks. The physical activity may remain split off from overall functioning. In this case, no real harm is done, but there will be no increase in somatic awareness. More seriously, if the defences are prematurely breached, the client may be overwhelmed by unmanageable psychic pain. I know of one case where engagement in bioenergetic exercises led to a psychotic episode, which in turn led to hospitalisation.

These considerations bring us face to face with the whole question of *being* and *doing*, and their relationship to each other. For better or for worse, psychoanalysis is a 'being with' kind of enterprise. It focuses on the provision of a particular kind of environment for the client and privileges a certain way of being with the client. An increase in somatic awareness, if it is achieved, is achieved through a process of inner consultation, reflection and dialogue. The material that emerges is told and re-told, so that over time links are made to other aspects of experience, to events in the past and to anticipated or imagined events in the future. In addition, although the psychoanalytic setting is initially strange to the client and the psychoanalytic relationship is different from any other relationship, the telling of a personal story is not a new and unfamiliar activity. It builds on the client's everyday conversations, which include both conversations with others and the unspoken conversations we all have with ourselves when we remember and reflect upon our experiences.

Through this process of reflection and dialogue, touch and movement activities that are already part of a client's life outside the consulting room come to be understood in a different way. Their relationship to the body storyline as a whole gradually becomes clearer. The client-led process of discovery usually leads to a change in the way in which current activities are experienced and used. An indirect outcome may be client-initiated engagement with new activities outside the therapy setting.

In this way, psychoanalysis adopts a low-risk strategy which respects the client's need for his or her defences and moves at the client's own pace. It is through his or her consistent concern for and attunement to the client's physical and psychological well-being, rather than through suggesting activities, that the psycho-analytic practitioner becomes midwife to the process of 'joining up' physiological and psychological aspects of experience. Clinical examples of these processes in action are presented in Part III of the book.

I will conclude this chapter by returning briefly to the distinc-tion between 'psychosomatic' and 'psychosocial' approaches to health. Both are important and may be seen as complementary lines of development. In recent years, psychosocial aspects of health have been recognised and engaged with in health care settings, particularly within the nursing profession. There has been a reappraisal of the patient's relationship with his or her carers and its role in healing. In Britain, for example, this has led to the prac-tice of assigning a 'named nurse' to each patient. In many hospi-tals, nurses have developed their counselling skills and incorporated them into nursing care. In a wider sense, the consid-eration of psychosocial health involves the consideration of a person's sense of belonging, the web of relationships and familiar rituals that guard against isolation and, it has been found, against ill-health (see, for example, Kobasa et al., 1985).

Psychosomatic health, on the other hand, refers to the indiv-idual's relationship to the aspect of himself that Orbach calls the 'corporeal self' (1995), to his subjective experience of indwelling within his own physicality. It also encompasses that part of the individual's internal world of associations and memories-in-feeling (Klein, 1957) which is specifically related to bodily experiences.

The various themes introduced in this chapter will re-emerge at various points as the book proceeds. During the long period, now seemingly coming to an end, when science and medicine asserted that health is a physical matter, determined by genes and environmental pathogens alone, our everyday language has continued to express the opposite view. A person's words may 'touch a raw nerve' or 'get under our skin'. These are just two of the many metaphors that attest in everyday language to the holistic and psychosomatic nature of our experience of living, both in sickness and in health.

# CHAPTER 4

# Science, Medicine and the Psyche-soma

Science as we have known it since the seventeenth century is about the detached, repeatable study of objective reality. Its whole credo rests on the exclusion of subjective phenomena, which follows from Descartes's clear distinction between the properties of mind and those of matter and from the later Newtonian preoccupation with matter as the proper object of scientific inquiry. (Marshall and Zohar, 1997: 109)

*Philosophers over the millennia have debated the question of 'mind and body' or 'embodied mind'. Although deliberations on the nature and significance of physicality date back considerably further, the account outlined here begins in the seventeenth century. It describes how the work of the eminent philosopher René Descartes set the scene for the age of modernism, the inexorable rise of science and the associated biomedical perspective on health and illness. The chapter continues with a consideration of the recent developments in psychology, particularly the development of health psychology, of the biopsychosocial perspective and of cognitive behavioural psychotherapy. It concludes with a discussion of contemporary perspectives in the neurosciences and some general comments on the growing influence of holistic perspectives over a very wide range of disciplines.*

## Science and dualism

Certain ideas that came to prominence in the seventeenth century have shaped, and to some extent continue to shape, perspectives on health and illness in contemporary Western society. René Descartes was responsible for the pronouncement that mind and body were separate entities, composed of different substances and

46

subject to different laws. He advocated different research methods for the two phenomena he had distinguished. The body, being a material object, could be explored via scientific investigation, but the mind was of a 'higher' order and could only be investigated by introspection.

Descartes was a devout Christian, and the philosophy of dualism (referring to the supposed 'dual' or two-fold nature of the human being) owed much to Christian theology and to the threat posed by early intimations of evolutionary theory to Man's special status in the universe. By splitting mind and body, it was possible to continue to regard human beings as fundamentally different from other members of the animal kingdom. Man had a soul; a monkey did not.

Premodern physicians, along with some of the ancient Greek and Hebrew philosophers, believed that states of mind were fundamentally entangled with physical health. In this sense, their approach was essentially 'holistic'. Dualism, on the other hand, encapsulated many of the features that became characteristic of the scientific method, including a belief in the possibility of absolute objectivity, an emphasis on linear cause and effect relationships and an embracing of reductionism. Descartes made explicit his 'reductionist' intention:

> to divide each difficulty I should examine into as many parts as possible, and as would be required the better to solve it. (Descartes, 1644)

Having split mind and body apart, philosophers have wrestled ever since with the problem of how these two (supposedly) separate entities affect one another, since clearly they *are* connected. The thought (mind) 'I would like to drink my coffee' is undeniably linked to the action (body) of moving my arm and picking up my cup. Recognising this, philosophers in the dualistic tradition have made many attempts to formulate a model of the interconnectedness between 'mind' and 'body'. One such model is that of psychophysical parallelism, which I single out for mention because it was the model adopted, albeit somewhat reluctantly, by Freud (1891). Readers who view the original division of one human being into separate parts as being fundamentally flawed will perhaps not be surprised to learn that efforts to bridge the resulting gap have failed to produce any generally accepted solution.

In spite of these unresolved philosophical issues, the scientific method based on a dualistic vision of the human being quickly became the dominant paradigm for conducting research, including medical research. Within this paradigm, there was a belief in the possibility of absolute objectivity and in the power of the scientific method to arrive at 'the truth'. Only results that were arrived at through the application of the scientific method and that lent themselves to quantitative analysis were considered to be of value.

Postmodern developments, described in the previous chapter, have ushered in a significant change in our understanding of what a 'science of the mind' might be. At the same time, science itself has changed, and there has been major re-thinking of some of its most fundamental tenets. At the cutting edge of contemporary science, it is accepted that the long-prized cause and effect model has a limited explanatory power. In its place, we have field theories, chaos theories and other complex ways of understanding events. These new models make much more modest claims in relation to eventual control and predictability. In addition, the cherished idea of total objectivity has been abandoned. Scientists now acknowledge that the observer always has an impact on the material observed, that topics chosen for research reflect a plethora of subjective elements, that political and materialistic considerations determine what research gets funded and that a single set of results lends itself to many different interpretations. (A valuable overview of these developments in scientific thinking for the lay reader can be found in *Who's Afraid of Schrödinger's Cat?* by Marshall and Zohar, 1997.)

In the heyday of modernism, it was generally believed that science would, through the conscientious application of the scientific method, provide the explanation for all phenomena. As the limitations of science have been revealed and the promise of constant progress has been understood to be unrealistic, public scepticism about science and about the value of some of its achievements has increased. This fall from grace of the 'God of Science' has dealt a significant blow to the primacy of modernism. In addition, postmodernism has spawned a damaging critique of the scientific claims, particularly with regard to the status of 'hard facts' and to the possibility of establishing general laws that hold good in all situations.

# The biomedical model of health

The biomedical model, bearing the hallmarks of dualism, concerns itself with the body as a separate and 'uninhabited' entity, apparently devoid of meaning and outside the influence of psychological factors. Psychiatrist and psychoanalyst Franz Alexander summed up the situation in the following way:

> The fundamental philosophical postulate of modern medicine is that the body and its functions can be understood in terms of physical chemistry, that living organisms are physicochemical machines and that the ideal of the physician is to become an engineer of the body. (Alexander, 1950: 18)

The biomedical model is characterised by the view that thoughts, feelings and imaginings belong to the mind and are not capable of affecting the body. There is a genuine belief that the physical aspects of the person can be understood without reference to the person as a whole – as a thinking, feeling subject shaped by and embedded within a particular social and cultural context. In addition, in order to gain better control of the many variables in play, there has been a tendency to focus on smaller and smaller subcategories of disease. This reductionism has been characteristic of all scientific approaches both within and outside the field of medicine. It is a characteristic also of behaviourism, the conceptual framework that dominated the field of psychology for many decades. Reductionism is falling from favour now, even in the 'hard' sciences such as physics, as science turns its attention to:

> the new properties and patterns that emerge when parts *combine* to form wholes. (Marshall and Zohar, 1997: xxvii)

Few of us would wish to deny the enormous improvement in health ushered in by the biomedical model. If many of our remaining major diseases have an obvious and substantial 'psychosomatic' component, this is in part because of the outstanding successes of Western medicine with regard to other, less psychologically shaped, illnesses. And although there is some evidence of the law of decreasing returns, advances continue to be made within the biomedical model. For example, I recently read that a micro-

tube has been developed, which can offer a pathway for the recon-
nection of two ends of a severed nerve. At present, children who
(for example) gash an arm badly and sever nerve fibres usually
suffer some permanent impairment of function. With this new
development, they can look forward to regaining the full use of the
affected arm and hand.

Western medicine in the biomedical mould has most to offer in
cases of illness in which psychological factors are at a minimum.
The involvement of psychological factors calls for a consideration
of the whole person, and not just the damaged tissue or the
bacterium or the virus. And it is in considering the whole person
that Western medicine reveals its most serious limitations. Where
the *context* of an injury or illness is centrally important, where the
whole person and his or her situation needs to be considered, the
biomedical model can part company with human compassion and
ordinary common sense.

A man in his 80s was diagnosed as having cancer of the jaw. This condition
was causing him only mild discomfort. He was strongly advised to undergo
major surgery, which would have removed about half of the lower part of his
face and left him unable to speak. With support from his family, he plucked
up the courage to say that he wanted radiotherapy treatment alone, without
surgery. The hospital consultant told him sternly that he could not possibly
sanction this course of action because it would reduce the chance of full
recovery from 75 per cent to 25 per cent. Only when this patient succeeded
in getting himself referred to a different medical establishment was his
decision to opt for less invasive treatment respected. Without his family's
support, there is little doubt that he would have capitulated and agreed to
the surgery that he did not want.

Many physicians, particularly those in less specialist areas of
medicine, find the biomedical perspective contradicted by their
everyday clinical experience. Terminally ill patients mysteriously
survive until they have spent one more Christmas with their families. A physician with a good 'bedside manner' gets better results
than one who is lacking in social skills. A strong 'will to live' can
considerably extend a patient's life. Although these effects are
known, anecdotal evidence suggests that they have not been fully
incorporated into the understanding of medical science and into

medical training. Fifty years ago, Franz Alexander commented on this same disjunction:

> Within the medical community, the practitioner can afford to assume a 'scientific' attitude which is essentially only a dogmatic antipsychological attitude. Because he does not know exactly how this psychic element works, because it is so contradictory to everything he has learned during his medical training, and because the recognition of the psychic factor seemingly disrupts the consistency of the physicochemical theory of life, such a practitioner tries to disregard the psychic factor as much as possible. As a physician, however, he cannot entirely disregard it. Confronted with his patients, his therapeutic conscience forces him to pay primary attention to this detested factor, the importance of which he instinctively senses. (Alexander, 1950: 23)

Attitudes are changing, and the changes that are in play have their sources both within and outside the medical profession. It is by no means unusual these days to find a physician pushing against the narrow strictures of the biomedical model (see, for example, Broom, 1997). According to their own report, a substantial minority of doctors, and a majority of nurses, now offer some form of complementary therapy as well as conventional medical treatment. Many surgeries now employ the services of an on-site counsellor.

This is, perhaps, just the beginning. An English physician in Brighton has 'prescribed' sessions at a local gym for patients with a range of conditions, including anxiety, stress and some heart conditions. A GP practice in Nottingham has begun to issue selected patients with vouchers for adult education classes: preliminary research has suggested that education is at least as effective as drugs in the treatment of depression. Hospices have introduced an array of complementary medicine options into their treatment programmes, and some health service Trusts have begun to employ osteopaths and aromatherapists, although the number involved is still very small. Recently, a student midwife at University College Hospital, London, told me that she was able to take a pregnant woman whose labour needed to be induced to see a health service acupuncturist in the same building. The acupuncturist was successful in getting the birth process started.

# The biopsychosocial model

Every week, new facts and figures emerge, adding further detail to our picture of the relationship between mental, physical and social aspects of health. As we enter the twenty-first century, most of us accept that an excess of emotionally demanding events, particularly if they are too closely spaced, is likely to be mirrored in an increased susceptibility to different kinds of illness. Many fields of study have contributed to the groundswell of opposition to dualism, to the division of a human being into two separate entities – 'mind' and 'body'. Challenges have come from a large number of disciplines, including sociology, philosophy, complementary medicine, nursing, the neurosciences and the new science of psychoneuroimmunology. One very significant development is the growing stature of the discipline of health psychology and of the associated biopsychosocial model of health.

The philosopher Thomas Kuhn (1962) used the term 'paradigm' (although he later preferred the phrase 'conceptual framework') to describe the overall framework of basic assumptions used by scientists as they analyse and interpret their data. A 'paradigm shift' involves a move to a fundamentally different way of seeing the world. After a certain period of stability, during which certain basic assumptions remain unquestioned, there is a relatively rapid shift in thinking, involving sweeping changes. The selection of research questions and the manner in which research is undertaken reflect this far-reaching shift. The rules of evidence, which dictate what is generally accepted as 'proof' and 'knowledge', also undergo fundamental change. The shift away from dualism and towards holism is recognised within health psychology as one of the major paradigm shifts of our times.

The associated biopsychosocial model is itself a part of this shift. It mounts an explicit challenge to the biomedical paradigm and the accompanying division of human beings into 'mind' and 'matter'. It questions the belief that medical research should be conducted as if the body were simply another kind of 'matter', as if the physical aspects of ourselves could stand alone as objects and yield their secrets without reference to the subjective 'mind'.

The biopsychosocial model offers a valuable context for experimental research and the findings that have so far emerged confirm our intuitive recognition that social conditions and psychological states are inextricably entangled with physical health. The development of the model also represents a clear break with behaviourism, which dominated the field of psychology for many decades. Behaviourism dismissed as 'unscientific' all evidence based on experience that could not be directly observed from the outside. What people said about their own experience was inadmissible as 'data'. Within the biopsychosocial framework, however, a person's description of his or her experience is accepted and valued. To give a flavour of the research taking place within this paradigm, I will summarise an example from *Health Psychology* by Sheridan and Radmacher (1992). It is suggested to a group of boys that their skin will be brushed with a leaf which produces an allergic rash. Their skin is brushed with a leaf from a harmless tree, but most of them nevertheless react with skin inflammation, which in some cases is quite severe. In the second stage of the study, the boys are told that their skin will be brushed with a leaf from a harmless tree. In fact, it is brushed with a leaf that is known to commonly produce a mild allergic reaction. None of the boys develops any skin inflammation.

The fall from favour of the behaviourist endeavour to 'cleanse' psychology of subjective elements brings the possibility of a closer collaboration between psychology and psychoanalysis. Studies such as the one outlined above offer 'hard' evidence of the inextricable entanglement of mental and physical aspects of the human subject. The phenomenon of suggestion is 'operationalised' and opened up for scientific study. A psychoanalytic approach offers a potentially complementary understanding of the internal processes at work in the individual translation of a suggestion from an authority figure into a physical change.

## Cognitive behavioural psychotherapy

I referred in the previous chapter to the burgeoning of complementary therapies, many of which have their roots in Eastern philosophy. We have seen an enormous growth in the popularity of practices such as acupuncture, yoga, t'ai chi and baby massage. But as far as the mainstream is concerned, we still have distinct 'health services' for physical illnesses and 'mental health services' for psychological illness, with very little integration between the two.

With the shift to a more holistic perspective within the discipline of psychology, criticisms of this situation have also been voiced by practitioners using a cognitive behavioural therapy approach. Some particularly interesting work has been done by the American psychologist Donal Bakal, who puts an increase in somatic awareness at the centre of his concerns. His work offers a valuable possibility for dialogue with the psychoanalytic fraternity, being very much in tune with comments made by Winnincott (1966) and others. Bakal sets out the following points:

> Medical intervention must include recognition of how intimately health is linked to attitudes, thoughts, feelings and behaviours.

> Scientific evidence cannot be ignored – who we are, where we live and how we think, feel and cope with bodily information can powerfully influence whether we get sick, how sick we get, and how best to manage our illness.

> Holistic patient management requires that patients not be sent to one 'repair shop' for sick thoughts and feelings and to another 'repair shop' for diseased organs. The mind and the body flourish or perish together.

> Patient care must shift to treating the whole person – the payoff will be healthier individuals, healthier communities, and a healthier nation. To do otherwise is irresponsible. (Bakal, 1999: 2)

In Britain, cognitive behavioural therapy enjoys a good reputation. As Bakal's work illustrates, there are a number of points of contact with psychoanalysis, with a number of assumptions and underlying understandings being shared by the two approaches. There are opportunities here for mutual gain, in spite of the significant differences in style of the practice, which are summarised below.

A cognitive behavioural approach involves the selection of a focus on one or two issues, and the therapist often actively structures and directs the therapy session. The theoretical underpinning of the work is learning theory, and the aim is for the client to question outmoded beliefs and assumptions and to learn more productive ways of seeing and thinking. Interestingly, in the case of *brief* psychoanalytic interventions, the psychoanalytic style is modified and moves much closer to the cognitive behavioural style, with a specific focus and goal usually being identified.

Broadly speaking, cognitive behavioural therapy focuses on behaviour while psychoanalytic psychotherapy focuses on understanding. But because behaviour and understanding are closely linked, the outcome achieved is likely to be more similar than one might imagine. When therapy seems to 'work', the question remains of which element of the encounter has had most influence on the change that has taken place. Cognitive behavioural practitioners believe that the particular techniques they employ, involving a structured approach to the consideration of thoughts and beliefs, are responsible for the therapeutic effect. Psychoanalytic practitioners place more emphasis on the relationship between client and therapist as the main agent of change.

It is probably important to reflect on the fact that people seek counselling or psychotherapy for a number of different reasons. Some are primarily concerned with *understanding* their behaviour while others find it more urgent to try to *change* their behaviour. The same difference of emphasis divides psychoanalytic from behavioural practitioners. It can, however, be argued that either approach, where successful, must result in both a change in self-understanding *and* a change in behaviour, for understanding is almost bound to transform an individual's behaviour. Instead of feeling 'all at sea', this individual can now chart a course that takes account of newly discovered wishes, hopes, fears and insights. For example, a woman may gradually uncover in psychoanalytic psychotherapy her motive for repeatedly returning to a man who abuses her. Now she has the possibility of addressing her needs in other ways. She is in a much stronger position to stop the abuse or to leave the relationship.

Similarly, a change of behaviour is almost bound to affect a person's self-understanding and understanding of the world. We might take the example of a person who has become unable to leave the house because of her fear of panic attacks. Through cognitive behavioural psychotherapy, she regains the capacity to go shopping or go to work or take the children to school. By this point, her self-concept must surely also have changed. Where she might have stated, 'I am not a confident person. My life is very curtailed', she can now say, 'I can take my place in the world and live a full life.' If feelings and self-concepts both influence and are influenced by behaviour, then the dichotomy between psychoanalytic and cognitive behavioural approaches is considerably less pronounced than is sometimes implied.

# Cause and effect

Although revolutionary in some respects, psychology approaches remain rather more committed than other holistic approaches to thinking in terms of 'cause and effect'. One aspect of the paradigm shift in progress resides in the challenge to the biomedical idea of an 'uninhabited' material body. A second and linked aspect involves a move away from thinking in terms of 'systems' and towards thinking in terms of 'stories' (Freedman and Combs, 1996). In contrast to these tendencies, research within psychology continues to centre on a quest for a 'root cause'. In the case of health, discussion is often focused on whether physical or psychological changes are 'primary'. The traditional scientific belief in the possibility of tracking down hard facts and basic causes is still in evidence. In principle, the biopsychosocial model allows room for the ideas of social construction and individual narrative construction of experience that are characteristic of the postmodern approach, but these have yet to find full expression.

If looking for a root cause sometimes makes sense, there are other occasions when it seems unnecessary and unhelpful. For example, a researcher asks whether the endorphins released when a person goes jogging 'cause' the typical feeling of well-being, or alternatively whether the experience of jogging 'causes' the feeling of well-being, which in turn 'causes' endorphins to be released. But this is perhaps an instance where the physiological and the psychological can be seen as simply two sides of the same coin, alternative descriptions of the same event. Like my typing of these words, the event – jogging that is enjoyed – has both a physiological and a psychological version. Similarly, a person who is provoked to anger may punch his desk, imagine himself striking out at an adversary, and feel the surge of blood to his face and the tensing of his muscles. These events are all of a piece. It makes no sense to think in terms of one aspect of the whole 'causing' the others.

Scientists often assume that physical and chemical realities are primary, and this assumption has fuelled a great deal of research into the supposed but elusive chemical or genetic roots of illnesses such as schizophrenia. Is such research worthwhile? Franz Alexander pointed out that, even when the physiological counterpart of a particular psychological phenomenon is better known, it is unlikely that we will be able to dispense with the psychological version:

It is hardly conceivable that the different moves of two chess players would ever be more clearly understood in biochemical or neurophysiological than in psychological terms. (1950: 55)

## Developments in the neurosciences

Although it presents a different kind of account of events, at the cellular level rather than at the level of subjective experience, research in the neurosciences has produced a number of interesting and relevant findings. Take, for example, a recent study which investigated the effectiveness of psychotherapy in treating depression. A report presented to the Royal College of Psychiatrists in London offered evidence from brain scans that six sessions of psychotherapy produced a significant increase in blood flow to specific areas of the brain. These measurable changes accompanied a subjectively experienced reduction in the symptoms of depression ('Why it's good to talk to a therapist', *The Times*, 1 July 1999).

*Descartes' Error* (1994), written by the eminent neurologist Antonio Damasio, both contributed to and confirmed the shift away from a dualistic framework in the neurosciences. Damasio's later work continues the development of a fruitful exchange with psychoanalysis, through the exploration of the neuroanatomy of consciousness. A unitary view of the human subject clearly emerges. Self-consciousness – defined as the self-referential aspect of consciousness – is described in terms of a:

> collection of nonconscious neural patterns standing for a part of the organism we call the body proper. (Damasio, 1999)

Damasio's argument is that our sense of individuality, of 'singularity of self', has its roots in the fact that we are embodied beings, *that we each inhabit only one body, which is not shared with any other human being.*

Olds and Cooper are among the psychoanalysts to have acknowledged the value of a dialogue between psychoanalysis and the neurosciences:

> Where once we were concerned about the reductionism of some forms of biology, today's biological forefront is based on hierarchical systems

theory, recognising emergent properties, and is unconcerned with trying to reduce poetic understanding to neuronal activity. (Olds and Cooper, 1997: 221)

In their 1997 paper 'Dialogue with other sciences: opportunities for mutual gain', these authors refer to the work of a number of different researchers. These include Edelman (1992), who presents evidence that the brain operates as a dynamic and integrated whole. Neurophysiologists have recently demonstrated that even a simple perception, such as seeing a cat, involves circuits that traverse the brain stem, limbic system and pre-frontal cortex. The overall picture that has emerged is that the development of neuronal circuits is heavily dependent upon the individual's experiences with the environment, in both its physical and its emotional aspects. Such a model of the brain and the influence of emotional and physical experiences on its evolution stands in sharp contrast to a dualistic model of body/mind (see Damasio, 1994).

## The rise and rise of holism

The basic subject is therefore a mental and physical subject–object physically extended in space. Hence, Cartesian dualism is inconsistent with a correct account of the nature and content of bodily awareness. (Brewer, in Bermudez et al., 1995: 303)

This quotation neatly summarises one of the main conclusions arrived at during a four-year joint philosophy and psychology Project on Spatial Representation, based at the King's College Research Centre in Cambridge.

As I hope I have made clear, contemporary shifts of thinking are by no means confined to academic circles. They influence and are influenced by many aspects of everyday living. They find expression particularly in the enormous interest in complementary health care and in health-enhancing practices such as yoga and t'ai chi. Indeed, much of the credit for the current popularity of the holistic paradigm must go not to academics or even to psychoanalysts but to the complementary therapists – massage therapists, homeopaths and many others – who are now such a major presence on the contemporary health care scene. In 1999, it was reported in the English press that more individual visits were made to complementary therapists than to general medical practitioners!

When considering holism, we must keep in mind the important aspect of the paradigm that denotes us as always being 'in the world' – a part of a larger whole – always 'embedded' as well as 'embodied'. This perception links to the psychoanalytic tradition of emphasising the absolute centrality of relationship, which was most strongly articulated by Melanie Klein. The emphasis on relationship remains a consistent feature of psychoanalytic approaches. One of Winnicott's well-known comments is that 'There is no such thing as a baby.' Expanding on this statement, Winnicott points out that when we see a baby, we also, in all normal circumstances, see the person caring for the baby, an activity which may involve simply holding the baby in mind. The baby and his care make up a whole. Later in life, our relatedness may be less visible, but it is always there. Even the concept of a 'hermit' – a person who does not relate to other human beings – is only meaningful against a background of human beings in relationship to others.

Contemporary psychoanalytic thinking places a strong emphasis on the processes by which early relationships become internalised, form a part of who we are and shape the ways in which we relate to new people in our lives. As well as participating in external relationships, psychoanalysis argues that we carry within ourselves a complex world of internal relationships, which both find expression in and are modified by our relationships with others in the present.

In the observation extracts and case studies that follow, I aim to flesh out the holistic psychoanalytic viewpoint. By offering detailed and practical accounts, these illustrative vignettes lend substance to theoretical understandings. They constitute the most powerful argument of all for seeing the human being as a unified whole, revealed in both the body and the word.

# CHAPTER 5

# Psychoanalysis and the Psyche-soma

Historically viewed, the development of psychoanalysis can be considered as one of the first signs of a reaction against the one-sided analytical development of medicine in the second half of the nineteenth century, against the specialized interest in detailed mechanisms, against the neglect of the fundamental biological fact that the organism is one unit and the function of its parts can only be understood from the point of view of the whole system. (Alexander, 1950: 33)

*In offering a perspective on human living as subjectively experienced, psychoanalysts have taken a number of different positions, not always explicitly stated, on the question of 'mind and body' or 'embodied mind'. To give an overview of these perspective in the brief envelope of a single chapter is a difficult task, one to which I have been persuaded only by frequent requests from students for a comparative summary. The account offered is necessarily selective – to do full justice to the complexities involved would require a separate book.*

## Metanarratives

The term 'narrative' refers not only to personal stories and histories, but also to theories, including theories of mind and body or embodied mind. We might think of these theories as 'metanarratives', offering an overview, a general perspective on the subject under consideration. Psychoanalytic metanarratives are derived primarily from the individual stories that have unfolded in clinical work. Psychoanalysts from different schools of thought share a core concern with early relationships, with unconscious dynamics and with the particular meanings that individuals bring to their experiences. Nevertheless, experiences encountered in the consulting room have been interpreted and theorised differently by different psychoanalytic writers. The theories set out below reflect some of these differences.

Because it evolved within a framework of dualistic assumptions, so universally accepted at the time that it was in effect invisible, early psychoanalytic theory was expressed in dualistic terms. As the Lacanians have shown, we are 'subject to' the language we are born into and to the social and political concerns folded into that language. At the same time, case study material runs counter to the assumptions of dualism and calls out for a more holistic reading. It is only recently, as phenomenological and postmodern perspectives have become more familiar, that the philosophical scene has been set for the potential resolution of these tensions.

## Sigmund Freud

On the basis of his successes with the 'talking cure', Freud was able to argue that some physical symptoms can be best understood in terms of unconscious mental conflict. In a logical extension of this argument, he asserted that we each have a part of ourselves of which we are not aware, an 'Unconscious' made up of the thoughts and feelings too uncomfortable to allow into consciousness. These repressed elements are not passive but 'dynamic'. They seek an outlet, emerging in symptoms, in dreams, in slips of the tongue or by insinuating themselves into our behaviour in ways that are invisible to us and outside our control.

Freud's work on the Unconscious epitomises his own questioning stance towards taken-for-granted knowledge. He saw his discovery of the Unconscious as being comparable to the Copernican discovery that the earth is not at the centre of the universe and the Darwinian discovery that we are descended from the animal kingdom:

> (But) human megalomania will have suffered its third and most wounding blow from the psychological research of the present time which seeks to prove to the ego that it is not even master in its own house, but must content itself with scanty information of what is going on unconsciously in the mind. (Freud, 1916: 326)

Freud's scepticism about what we assume we know is not easy to reconcile with his developmental and topographical models of human functioning, which are at times presented as factual accounts with universal applicability.

Freud's work on the libido, source of sexual desire and creativity, lies at the heart of his project. In developmental terms, he suggests that the libido develops on the basis of the physiological functions associated with various erogenous zones – oral, anal, phallic and genital. Erotic pleasures and desires are first attached to the actions of sucking and biting and the fantasies associated with them. A year or so later, they become centred on urinating and defecating and finally, much later, they move on to the genital activity. The main focus of libidinal energy shifts from one erogenous zone to another as the organism matures.

In his 'topographical' account, Freud describes the libidinal drive as running counter to the requirements of civilised living. These requirements are communicated in the form of parental attitudes and behaviour, eventually being internalised within the individual as the 'super-ego' or conscience. The implicit dualism of this account is evident, the physically based drives of the 'id' being set in opposition to those of the psychologically based super-ego. The 'ego' (literally the 'I') has the role of mediation. It is 'a frontier creature, endeavouring to facilitate traffic and trade' (Freud, 1923) between id and super-ego. Sometimes the ego performs this task with considerable panache. At other times, it is overwhelmed, and a person becomes neurotic or otherwise ill. Freud describes human beings as faced from early on with the task of finding a means of expression of their libidinous drives – in accordance with the 'pleasure principle' – and at the same time conforming to the 'reality principle' (Freud, 1911) of social expectations. The conflict between the pleasure principle and the reality principle becomes more onerous as a person matures.

Freud denotes the id (literally the 'it') as the well-spring of instinctual drives, as body based. Interestingly, he also describes the ego as 'first and foremost a bodily ego' (Freud, 1923). He suggests that the early development of the ego depends on a sense of the skin, which forms a boundary between the inner and outer worlds of the individual. Thus, the significance of the skin, which is an important topic in later psychoanalytic writing, was first raised for consideration by Freud.

As a philosophical underpinning for his work, Freud nominally subscribed to a version of dualism known as 'psychophysical parallelism' (Freud, 1891). Neville Symington is a contemporary psychoanalyst who has questioned this decision:

> Freud's view is that the drives have a somatic source – a source in the body – which is then paralleled in the psyche.
>
> Psycho-physical parallelism does not seem to me to be a satisfactory philosophical account of the human entity. I think that man is a single entity, not composed of body and soul in parallel with each other. (1986: 134)

It can be argued that, from the very beginning, Freud's work sat uncomfortably within his adopted framework. His case study narratives highlighted the extraordinary complexities of mind/body entanglement. In addition, rather than proposing a simple cause and effect relationship between 'mind' and 'body', Freud argued that symptoms are always 'over-determined'. By this he meant that any number of different circumstances and influences may combine to produce a single symptom, and that one single cause is never enough to result in illness.

Freud's account has had a mixed reception. Scientists complain that his hypotheses do not meet the conventional requirements of the scientific method. Until recently, many physicians derided the idea that the psychological and the physiological are entwined in such a way that difficult emotional circumstances can find expression in physical symptoms. In the straight-laced Viennese society of the 1890s, Freud's cause was not helped by his view (later disputed by Jung) that all psychosomatic symptoms had their origins in repressed *sexual* desires, kept out of mind because of their shameful and disturbing nature. The idea of childhood sexuality was found to be particularly shocking.

In recent times, Freud has been criticised in some quarters for his insistence, particularly in his early work, on the 'scientific' nature of his discoveries. Some writers have argued that psychoanalysis is not a science and should not be presented as such. Like great literature, it offers a non-scientific way of understanding human experience. A new twist to the debate has arisen from our shifting understanding of what we might understand by the term 'science'. In an unforeseen turn of events, science itself is being forced to reassess many of its claims, for example of objectivity and of measurement that is not affected by the person doing the measuring. At the cutting edge, scientific understandings have moved closer towards Freud's way of thinking.

Freud faced many difficulties in establishing psychoanalysis as a discipline and as a profession. In order to stand any chance of acceptance among the medical researchers and physicians who dominated the late nineteenth-century landscape of ideas, he would have been *obliged* to present psychoanalysis as a science. If it can be said that Freud stayed formally within the tenets of the biomedical model, it can equally be said that his work constantly subverted the assumptions of that same model. Putting psychosomatics on the map in the most inauspicious of circumstances, at a time when the biomedical model reigned supreme, remains one of Freud's major achievements.

## Carl Jung

An important area of difference between Freud and Jung resides in their respective views on the cause of neurosis. While Freud believed that the repression of sexual thoughts and feelings was always involved, Jung took a much broader view. It is apparent that there were also differences of perspective on the issue of 'mind' and 'body'. Jung believed that body and spirit were simply different aspects of the reality of the psyche.

Jung and Reich (see below) both started out as disciples of Freud but later went their own ways in the wake of painful disputes and schisms. Jung was to develop his ideas primarily in relation to the spiritual aspect of the psyche. Reich concentrated on the body aspect of the psyche. In the end, each of these two very different characters developed a distinctive perspective on the psyche-soma.

Jung arrived at a complex model of the human subject, which differs from Freud's in a number of important respects. As in the case of Freudian theory, many aspects of Jung's work fall outside the scope of this chapter. Most relevant to the subject of health is Jung's perspective on physicality. This reveals itself over the course of his writing as an aspect of his strongly developed interest in spirituality, an interest that eventually led him to the study of Eastern philosophy and its associated practices, such as kundalini yoga.

Jung's ability to move explicitly outside the dualistic framework of Western philosophy owes a great deal to this involvement with Eastern philosophy.

Jung set his account against the background of nearly two thousand years of Christianity, a religion which advocates the mortification of the flesh and the renunciation of the instincts in the interests of spiritual development. He argued that setting spirit and physicality in opposition to one another would lead to an eventual crisis.

> The fascination of the psyche brings about a new self-appraisal, a reassessment of our fundamental human nature. We can hardly be surprised if it leads to a rediscovery of the body after its long subjugation to the spirit – we are even tempted to speak of the body's revenge on the spirit. (Jung, 1933: 253)

In the Jungian account, health resides primarily in a successful process of individuation. Individuation involves bringing to consciousness all the various aspects of the self, including those which we would prefer not to know about, designated by Jung as the 'shadow'. The integration of the shadow is an ongoing task, essential to our full development. In the passage below, Jung links the shadow to the body:

> The body is a most doubtful friend because it produces things we do not like; there are too many things about the body which cannot be mentioned. The body is very often the personification of this shadow of the ego. Sometimes it forms the skeleton in the cupboard, and everybody naturally wants to get rid of such a thing. (Jung, 1956 cited in Blackmer Dexter, 1989)

Skeletons in the cupboard tend to cause a great deal of trouble. Efforts to conceal them create considerable tension, and there is a danger that physicality will make its reappearance in a distorted form, perhaps as a psychosomatic symptom or an eating disorder or an act of self-harm.

I mentioned earlier the close association that has developed between Jungian theory and art, movement and dance therapies. Jungian thinking has provided a particularly fertile source of ideas to explore what dance teacher and psychotherapist Joan Blackmer Dexter (1989) refers to as 'the extraordinary potency of the psyche to animate the body'. Blackmer Dexter offers an example of such

animation when she describes her efforts to teach dance students
'how to carry the head with a fluidity and balance which is at once
controlled and free':

> Once, when I was searching for a way to get this across to a class, the
> unconscious spontaneously gave me an image: 'Hold your head as if
> you were carrying antlers.' It worked! (1989: 69)

This example links to another important theme developed by
Jung concerning the balance of introversion – a focus on inner
sensations – and extraversion – a focus on the external world.
Blackmer Dexter refers to the need to balance an *extraverted orientation* towards the reflection of the body in a mirror with an *intro-
verted orientation* towards the inner feeling of what happens when
one adopts a certain physical position. This latter brings fully into
play the sense of proprioception, referred to in Chapter 1, through
which we have an internal sense of the position and speed of movement of the body and its parts.

There are a number of areas of overlap between Jungian and
Winnicottian thinking. Both set great store by the process of individuation, arising out of an inborn tendency to, as Winnicott put it,
'become the person one was meant to become'. But whereas in
Jung's work, this sometimes sounds like a lone venture, Winnicott
always emphasises the context of relationship, within which the
individuation process finds its particular form. Both Jung and
Winnicott argue that the specialised mental function of thinking
remains, in health, continuous with physical self-awareness, the
latter serving as a source of natural wisdom, spontaneity and
energy. Any disturbance of this continuity is linked in both
accounts to experiences of dissociation and depersonalisation.

A Jungian perspective includes the suggestion that a return to
health may require the *physical use of the body* and *tactile contact* as
well as a process of *psychological exploration*. However Jungians do
not assume, as bodywork therapists seem to, that the physical and
psychological aspects of recovery need to be worked with in the
same arena. In fact, Blackmer Dexter argues explicitly in favour of
a separation of time and place between the two:

> But the real body work, the consistent, laborious process of differenti-
> ating and awakening the body, needs in my experience to be done sepa-
> rately, outside of the consulting room.

In the physical training arena one learns by doing. In the analytic hour one tries to discover what the doing means psychologically and symbolically. (1989: 112)

This model, involving one arena for engaging with movement and touch and a second area for being with and reflecting on these experiences, is central to the 'working with body storylines' approach, described later in Part III.

## Wilhelm Reich and body psychotherapy

Wilhelm Reich was a student of Freud's friend and colleague, Sandor Ferenczi. Although Ferenczi's well-known experiments with 'active techniques' strained his relationship with Freud, he succeeded in remaining within the psychoanalytic circle. Georg Groddeck too, although he announced himself as 'the wild analyst', was defended by Freud against other analysts who found his work too controversial. Reich, however, pushed the grand master too far. Totton (1998) describes how Reich was rather ruthlessly and secretively expelled from the International Psychoanalytic Association in 1934.

Although Freud may have treated Reich harshly, his fear that Reich would bring psychoanalysis into disrepute seems to be not entirely without foundation. Some of Reich's methods, for example measuring his experiments with Geiger counters, laid psychoanalysis wide open to the charge of 'quackery'. Reich's later conception of collective sexual energy and of a cosmic energy field, described as an 'orgone ocean', are other ideas that have fallen by the wayside, having met with little enthusiasm either within or outside psychoanalysis.

One of Reich's enduring contributions resides in the idea that body positions typical of our relationships with others in childhood – for example, the shrinking away of a child who thinks he is likely to be hit – become frozen in the body as 'character structures' or 'character attitudes':

The entire world of past experience is embodied in the present in the form of character attitudes. A person's character is the functional sum of all past experiences. (Reich, 1942: 145)

Reich's developmental account is in some respects similar to Freud's description of the oral, anal, phallic and genital stages. According to both theories, development can become arrested at any stage, and this will result in a characteristic personality tendency or pathology.

A linked aspect of Reichian theory resides in the description of the development of a 'body armour' (Reich, 1945). Reich attaches considerable importance to the role of the musculature in keeping alive the effects of repression. Freud has described the effects of repressing disallowed thoughts, feelings and impulses in terms of a distortion and rigidity of personality. Reich adds to that account, arguing that repression is also biologically grounded, taking the physical form of muscular rigidity:

> It can be said that every muscular rigidity contains the history and meaning of its origin. (Reich, 1945: 30)

Reich and his pupil Alexander Lowen link the origins of muscular rigidity to early experiences of holding the breath and tensing the muscles in order to suppress unbearable or unacceptable feelings and impulses. These accounts link to the phenomenon of body memory, with which psychotherapists, particularly those working with people suffering from post-traumatic stress disorder, are well acquainted.

Reich used a particular kind of deep massage in his work, believing that he could work directly with the muscular tension and the flow of energy. He did not consider verbal exploration to be a necessary part of the therapeutic process:

> Reichian therapists who call themselves 'body-therapists' close out the psyche in their definition, since one can in their opinion work directly with energy flow. (Boadella, 1998: 263)

This is an interesting twist on the phenomenon of dualism. Whereas verbal psychotherapy sometimes overlooks the importance of the physical domain, Reichian psychotherapy has its own blind spot, in so far as it disregards the importance of verbal and other symbolic processes. Contemporary bodywork approaches continue to draw on Reich's work but give more weight to certain aspects of a mainstream psychoanalytic approach. This provides the basis for a *rapprochement* and a greater sharing of ideas across the boundaries of the two fields. Contemporary bodywork psychotherapist Michael Soth writes:

> The body-oriented tradition has moved a long way from the 70s emphasis on discharge and cartharsis and has more to offer than a set of techniques. It shares with the psychodynamic perspective a focus on the relationship dynamic in terms of transference and countertransference. (1999: 6)

Bodywork psychotherapist Bernd Eiden (1998) has contributed a thoughtful discussion on the issue of touch, both inside and outside the psychotherapy setting. He points out that we all have a history of touch experiences and that these experiences fundamentally affect our health. His point of view concurs in all major respects with the one being put forward here. Touch is an area of experience that is inevitably worked with in some way in a psychotherapeutic encounter, whether through direct physical contact or through the verbal exploration of body storylines.

While the ideas that have evolved within psychoanalytic and bodywork therapy overlap to some degree, the techniques have remained distinct. Psychoanalytic psychotherapists do not include touch techniques within their approach and most of them discourage informal physical contact. Instead, they work verbally and, for the most part intuitively, with symbolic equivalents of touch, such as tone of voice or quality of gaze.

## Melanie Klein

Melanie Klein and her colleagues retained the Freudian notion of physically based instincts or drives, but Klein modified Freud's account in important ways. First, she gave a much more central position to the operation of the death drive, expressed in aggressive, destructive and envious impulses. Second, she asserted that the conflict between different drives was played out in a context of relatedness from the very beginning of life. The earliest relationship to the mother is elevated to a position of very great importance in Kleinian theory. Klein believed that human beings struggle from the start with a constitutionally based conflict between the forces of love and hate, played out in the first instance within the mother–infant relationship.

According to Klein, the shape and colouring of these experiences is internalised and forms the basis of 'internal objects', experienced as substantial and almost tangible aspects of the self. An internal object may be benign, for example an internal 'good mother', in which case it serves as a psychological resource for the individual. Alternatively, it may be hostile or persecutory and undermine healthy functioning.

Through her work with infants and children, Klein came to believe that an infant does not initially recognise his mother as a whole person with needs and wishes of her own. He treats parts of her, most importantly the breast, as 'objects'; thus, the term 'object relations' arose out of this understanding. The idea of fantasies (particularly the unconscious fantasies described as 'phantasies') being woven around our activities and experiences from the earliest days of our being lie at the core of Kleinian theory. Nick Totton writes that:

> In one sense, Kleinian analysis is very body-focused; many of its central terms and concepts derive from early bodily experiences. But it is the body *image*, the body as taken up and transformed through mental phantasy, on which Kleinian theory focuses, and this is a very different (and very important) topic. The fleshly body, it seems to me, does not appear in Klein. (1998: 6)

I am inclined to question the distinction made here between the body elaborated in phantasy and the 'fleshly' body, for are they not one and the same? We all know, for example, that both conscious and unconscious fantasy can find a very 'fleshly' form, for example when sexual fantasies or dreams lead to the bodily changes associated with sexual arousal. Klein argued, however, that there was further elaboration to be taken into account. She suggested, for example, that when a child has an easy or a difficult feed, the mother's breast may be experienced as 'generous' or as 'withholding'. When the child is hungry and is not fed, the breast may be envied for apparently having and keeping all the milk for itself. In making sense of the disturbed behaviour of the children she treated through psychotherapy, Klein discovered that such phantasies form the basis of internal objects and continue to colour our relationships in adult life.

Klein, who was 'inspired to watch and listen to the detail of small children at play' (Miller et al., 1989), ushered in a shift of emphasis within psychoanalysis, particularly in Britain, towards a level of theorising much closer to actual clinical observations. She also had a very straightforward and physically grounded basis for judging the effectiveness of her interventions. During her clinical sessions, she watched to see whether an interpretation she made was followed by a freeing up of the child's play. If there was a reduction in anxiety and inhibition in play, this indicated to Klein that the work was moving along the right lines.

## Object relations theory

The contemporary object relations umbrella within psychoanalysis includes both post-Kleinian work and the work of the British Independent group, including the work of Winnicott. In terms of both theory and practice, there are also areas of substantial overlap with self-psychology as it has evolved in the USA. Within this broad church, a number of different perspectives on the question of physicality are represented. Some psychoanalysts remain attached, at least in their theoretical formulations, to dualistic assumptions. This position is exemplified in the early work of the highly respected psychoanalyst Joyce McDougall, although her later work offers a rather different picture. The framework set out below is explicitly dualistic:

> At this point we come back to the fact that the mental and the physical are indissolubly linked yet at the same time essentially different. (McDougall, 1974: 441)

McDougall is then faced with the same dilemma that has tested philosophers for hundreds of years. If psyche and soma are, as Descartes asserted, 'separate and composed of different substances', what is the nature of the connection between them? McDougall's solution is to compare the psyche-soma to 'a fusional substance like sea-water':

> In spite of its unity our sea-water can be transformed on the one hand into a heap of dried salts and on the other, a cloud of watery vapour.

Let us say that the somatic elements are the salts and the psychic dimension the watery cloud. This allows us to conceive the two components
as different in substance and subject to different laws. (1974: 443)

Winnicott's work illustrates the opposite end of the continuum,
offering an explicitly holistic perspective. His view of the psyche-
soma stands in opposition to the idea that a human being is made
up of two different elements, such as salt and water vapour, which
are 'subject to different laws'. For Winnicott, the psyche-soma is, in
health, an indivisible unity. The appearance of a 'duality psyche-
soma' is seen as a consequence of defensive splitting in the face of
'impingements' from the environment that cannot be managed in
other ways. Thus, the split that does sometimes develop *in extremis*
is not normal: it is a result of trauma. Once enacted, it paves the
way for those 'mysterious leaps' from mind to body, which some
psychosomatic specialists still take as their starting point.

Winnicott moves away from the Kleinian emphasis on conflict
between different forces within the individual. Although he
acknowledges the value of Klein's insights into the inner world of
the infant, he makes it clear that, in his view, Klein paid too little
regard to the external environment. Winnicott considered the real
environment to be crucially important, particularly during the
early weeks of life when the infant is in a state of almost absolute
dependency. This dependency is 'psychosomatic', involving a need
both to be held in mind and to be physically handled:

For Winnicott, there was the body at the root of development out of
which a 'psychosomatic partnership' evolved. The self was first and foremost a body self and the 'psyche' of the partnership 'means the imaginative elaboration of somatic parts, feelings and functions, that is, of
physical aliveness'. (Phillips, 1988: 78)

The field of object relations has seen the development and elaboration of the concepts of transference and countertransference.
The complex debate that has taken place is outside the scope of
this summary. We may take these terms to refer in a general sense
to the client's feelings towards the therapist and the therapist's
feelings towards the client. Some of these feelings arise from situations and relationships outside the consulting room, which are
'transferred' on to the relationship between therapist and client.

Many of the feelings and attitudes involved are unconscious, but they may be brought into conscious awareness through the psychotherapy process.

Some analysts have argued that it is artificial to separate out transference and countertransference. American psychoanalyst, William Ogden, who has carried forward and developed some of Winnicott's most important theoretical contributions, has linked what he calls 'the transference–countertransference matrix' to Winnicott's idea of a 'transitional space' between mother and baby. This transitional space, also referred to as a 'third other', in the room is an area of experiencing that belongs to neither of the parties, yet is contributed to and experienced by both:

> I do not view transference and countertransference as separable entities that arise in response to one another; rather, I understand these terms to refer to aspects of a single intersubjective totality experienced separately (and individually) by analyst and analysand. (Ogden, 1997: 25)

The 'third other' can make itself felt in many ways, including in physical sensations. We may be aware of this effect – perhaps taking the form of a headache or a nauseous feeling – in everyday conversations that feel in some way tense or awkward, although the source of the 'charge' in the air is unclear. In the psychotherapy setting, such sensations, understood as unconscious-to-unconsicous communications, can help to illuminate the process in play between client and therapist. Psychoanalyst Nathan Field described experiences of sleepiness, sexual arousal and fear and trembling in the context of work with different clients:

> Miss A comes to mind in this regard. Her manifest manner was unfailingly bright, as she relentlessly entertained me with stories of people she knew while resisting every attempt to reach her underlying feelings... The effect on me was as if I was forcibly anaesthetised.

> Even more distressing than my struggle against acute drowsiness was the accompanying sense of bleakness and utter depletion. Even on the warmest day I felt impelled to switch on the fire, so drained and chilled did I feel. (1989: 514)

Field considers these experiences in terms of an 'embodied countertransference', which he characterises as:

> a kind of internalised body language that offers an additional means of access to primitive levels of communication. (1989: 513)

In the case of Miss A, he eventually concludes that he has been required to endure, without retaliating, the client's primary hatred for her mother.

One of the key aspects of psychoanalytic work with body story-lines is attending to embodied aspects of the transference–countertransference matrix. I shall return to this subject in Part III of the book, where individual pieces of clinical work are presented and discussed.

# Part II

## Infant Observation Studies

# CHAPTER 6

# Psychoanalytic Infant Observation

The physical sensations and experiences of a baby are seen as part of a unified continuum of physical and mental states. The significance for observer of a baby's sense of physical togetherness, or panic, or attachment through sucking (or biting) to the mother, is that it is expressive of a baby's whole state of mind/body, not a physical action alone. (Rustin, in Miller et al., 1989: 62)

*This chapter offers an introduction to psychoanalytic infant observation. Areas of complementarity with the work of D.W. Winnicott, the intersubjectivists and the post-Kleinian practitioners who inaugurated and developed the theory and practice of psychoanalytic infant observation are outlined and discussed.*

In the late 1960s, post-Kleinian analysts Esther Bick and Martha Harris introduced a two-year period of infant observation into the child psychotherapy training programme at the Tavistock Clinic in London. Over time, a period of psychoanalytic infant or child observation has become a relatively familiar feature of psychoanalytic psychotherapy training and, to a lesser degree, of social work and health visitor training.

Students often experience observation as a special and valuable form of learning. For an hour of each week, the student enters into the infant's everyday environment. He or she is a very unusual kind of guest: a stranger at first, yet privileged to witness and live through some of the pleasures and difficulties that are a part of every child's development and every family's adaptation to a new arrival.

One theme which repeatedly emerges concerns the experiences, common to all infants, of being mentally or physically 'dropped'

and also of being 'gathered together'. Such experiences are
revealed as playing a key role in early development. In Winnicott's
terms, they seem to be crucial to the quality of the 'indwelling of
the psyche in the soma', which may become either robustly or only
feebly established, depending both on the constitutional make-up
of the infant and the circumstances that he or she encounters. The
value of observation in training is now widely recognised. It
provides a rich opportunity for a practitioner to refine his or her
sensitivity to and understanding of minute-to-minute changes in
feeling states.

## Psychoanalytic infant observation as a research method

The status of qualitative research has risen as the scientific goal of
research untainted by subjective factors has been acknowledged to
be spectacularly elusive (see Chapter 3). In recent years, this kind
of observation has begun to be used as a tool of psychoanalytic
research as well (see Briggs, 1997; Reid, 1997). In contrast to other
methods of research into infant and child development, the
method of psychoanalytic infant observation is both naturalistic
and longitudinal. This is in keeping with the psychoanalytic understanding that a close examination of individual clinical cases yields
as much information as surveys or questionnaires. The information
that is gathered is of a different and less general nature than data
emanating from quantitative research and in this lies its particular
value. Psychoanalytic infant observation eschews any claim to
objectivity. Although the observer is there only to observe, his or
her impact on the situation is explicitly acknowledged:

> Although required to refrain from initiating activity and interaction, he
> is expected to maintain a friendly and receptive attitude to the family,
> of whom he is a privileged guest. ...It is in any event not possible to be
> an observer in a family and not be noticed, or to have no impact on the
> family system. (Briggs, 1997: 27)

In many respects, the structure of an observation echoes the
structure of a psychotherapy. There are similarities, for example, in
the regularity and duration of the visits, the special role of the

observer and the considerable duration of the observation period, which is usually two years. As with the psychotherapy hour, the content of the observation hour is 'client led', structured by the family with the observer fitting in around whatever takes place. While each observed infant is individual and particular, pattern and meaning do emerge over time as certain themes appear and reappear in different contexts.

Observations are recorded in everyday language, with the aim of describing the immediate realities of the situation. Rather than applying theoretical categories or interpretations, observers open themselves to the situation and then make a written record of what they see and what they feel. Later, in a small seminar group, which has parallels with the psychotherapist's regular supervision session, the observations are discussed. At this stage, links to existing theory may be made, and new ideas may emerge. In keeping with the narrative approach outlined earlier, none of the suggestions I make when considering the observation extracts presented is intended to rule out other versions, other interpretations of what went on. This constant holding in mind and juxtaposition of alternative hypotheses is characteristic of the spirit of the weekly seminar group where the observations of the participants are presented and discussed.

## Winnicott and observation

The evolution of the method of psychoanalytic infant observation overlapped with the later years of Winnicott's life. Winnicott had long held observation in high esteem:

> What do we depend on to make us feel alive, or real? Where does our sense come from, when we have it, that our lives are worth living? Winnicott approached these issues through the observation – one of his favoured words – of mothers and infants, and what became in time the 'transitional space' between them. (Phillips, 1988: 5)

Winnicott's observations were mostly of an informal nature, although some were undertaken in a 'set situation' (Winnicott, 1941). They were undertaken in the context of his work as a paediatrician, which involved him in encounters with literally thousands

of mother–infant pairs. Winnicott seemed to have a special sensitivity to relationships between babies and their mothers, and this
enabled him to develop a particular understanding of the delicate
mechanisms that underpinned and shaped these relationships.
Perhaps because of his ongoing day-to-day contact with 'ordinary'
families through his paediatric work, Winnicott always managed to
keep at least half an eye on health. He cautioned more than once
against the tendency inherent in psychoanalysis (and in any profession that deals mainly with people who are ill) to view behaviour
too readily in terms of pathology.

## Heredity and environment

The relative influence of hereditary and environmental factors in
human behaviour is a theme that has long been researched and
debated in the field of psychology. Theories advanced on the basis
of particular interpretations of research results have been adopted
to support political positions on both the Left and the Right. In
general, an emphasis on environmental factors has been used by
the Left to argue that social conditions are at the root of deviant
behaviour and of poor performance, both at school and in life
generally. An emphasis on hereditary factors has been used by the
Right to justify the dominant position of white people (on the
basis of their supposedly superior intellectual endowment) and to
argue for children to be segregated into different kinds of school
on the basis of ability. The contemporary phenomenon of 'evolutionary psychology' embodies a similarly deterministic position,
albeit framed in a new terminology. In recent years, in a welcome
development, the more moderate view that constitutional and
environmental factors interact in such a complex way that we
cannot attribute relative values to the influence of each has gained
greater acceptance.

For many years, psychoanalysis was also the scene of a debate
between those who supported Klein's very strong focus on constitutionally determined internal conflicts and those who supported
Winnicott's view of a more equal conjunction of constitutional and
environmental factors. A process of gradual *rapprochement* has come
to fruition in the arena of psychoanalytic infant observation. The
process of observation gives full weight *both* to the environment,

which includes all aspects of maternal care, *and* to what the infant brings to and does with that environment. As a consequence of this synthesis, it has become possible to include both the external provision and Kleinian insights into the infant's creation and use of that provision within the same frame. The 'observed infant' can be seen to be both dependent on the external environment and engaged from the first moments of life in eliciting that environment and making something of it.

## Psychoanalysis and developmental psychology

Up until the 1970s, psychology research in the area of infant development involved bringing an infant into a special setting, a kind of 'laboratory' to be tested on a pre-set task. The experimental task might involve distinguishing between a mother's voice and a stranger's voice (by sucking harder on a specially wired-up teat to obtain the preferred voice) or showing a preference for either a face or a coloured pattern (by looking at one for longer than at the other). For the research task to be undertaken, the infant needed to be in a state of 'alert inactivity'. (A distressed, excited or distracted infant cannot, by definition, attend properly to a pre-set task.)

Within its limitations, this kind of research has been very successful and has in many ways transformed our understanding of the human infant. The myth of the infant who cannot see clearly and whose sense impressions are disconnected and chaotic has been largely dispelled (see, for example, Bower, 1977):

> The more the perceptual world of the young infant is investigated, the more competent the infant seems to be. (Bower, 1989: 24)

This kind of research tends to focus on cognitive functioning and perceptual capacities and to screen out the consideration of emotional states. Notwithstanding the value and interest of the work, it is rather limiting to study an infant only in a state of 'alert inactivity'. Because of the importance we attach to the inner world of emotion and phantasy, psychoanalysts have sometimes felt that research of this kind misses what is most important about an infant's experience (see Bradley, 1989).

The 'intersubjectivists', operating at the interface of developmental psychology and psychoanalysis, thought carefully about this limitation and inaugurated a different research approach. The best known figure, Daniel Stern, stated a desire to research what he described as a 'clinically relevant baby'. Rather than conducting research into an infant's performance on pre-set tasks, Stern and other intersubjectivists, including Brazelton, Trevarthen and Beebe, began to make video recordings of mother–infant interactions as they transpired. A painstaking frame-by-frame analysis of the resulting videos completed the research procedure, and a fascinating and detailed picture of the early attunement and rhythmic interaction of mother and baby began to emerge.

In common with other 'realities' or 'facts', what is observed lends itself to a number of different interpretations. The narratives constructed by the intersubjectivists differ in some respects from post-Kleinian and Winnicottian accounts. Stern objects to Klein's statements on the existence of infant phantasies, because they cannot be demonstrated, and to Winnicott's suggestion that mother and baby experience themselves as intermittently merged in the early weeks of the infant's life. More significant, however, are the areas of overlap and complementarity. Klein suggested, and Winnicott agreed, that infants were born with a certain sociability, a readiness to relate to others, albeit in a primitive way:

> I have seen babies as young as three weeks interrupt their sucking for a short time to play with mother's breast or look towards her face. (Klein, 1952: 152)

This view is confirmed by the intersubjectivists' work. All of the key figures refer at times to the early sociability of the human infant. Trevarthen (1979), for example, states that 'a human is born with the readiness to know another human'.

A shared interest in relatedness and changing emotional states has fostered a two-way process of communication between the post-Kleinian and intersubjectivist strands. A particularly valuable contribution from the intersubjectivists has been the detailed mapping of the 'dance' of interaction between mother and baby, the 'conversational' rhythm of their early exchanges and (when all is going well) the exquisite timing of their interactions:

The infant is a virtuoso performer in his attempts to regulate both the level of stimulation from the caregiver and the internal level of stimulation in himself. The mother is also a virtuoso in her moment-by-moment regulation of the interaction. Together they evolve some exquisitely intricate dyadic patterns. It takes two to create these patterns, which sometimes look ominous for the future and sometimes look quite effortlessly beautiful. (Stern, 1977: 121)

The technique of microanalysis of video footage is in many ways complementary to the practice of psychoanalytic infant observation. Both methods testify to the centrality of the emotional and relational world of the infant. Microanalysis provides a very detailed record, which can be viewed again and again, and which is an invaluable teaching aid. Psychoanalytic infant observation provides a longitudinal record of an infant in his or her natural setting and follows the development of that same individual into childhood. The seminar group provides an important site for reflection, both on the impact of the observer on the observed situation and on the emotional impact of the situation on the observer. The observer's personal experience of 'being there' is seen as vital to the overall understanding of what is going on.

## Infant health and handling

According to Winnicott, each of us has an inherited tendency to achieve and maintain a unity of psyche and soma, described as:

an *experiential identity* of the spirit or psyche and the totality of physical functioning. (1966: 112)

The flowering of this inherited tendency is dependent upon experiences of emotional 'holding' and responsive human touch or 'handling'. Experiences of handling are described by Winnicott as a crucial aspect of maternal care, with far-reaching consequences for infant and adult health. This point of view is widely accepted. Psychologists, health visitors, social workers and many other professionals with an interest in health recognise what is self-evident to the ordinary 'good enough' mother. Babies and children have a non-negotiable need for responsive human touch.

Winnicott suggests that good enough experiences of handling usher in a good quality of indwelling, consolidating the unity of the psyche-soma and supporting a development of mental functioning that is rooted in the experience of proper embodiment and hence of full emotionality. The alternative, where handling is not good enough, involves the activation of primitive defences. One such defence involves the splitting off of mental functioning from the overall functioning of the psyche-soma:

> Certain kinds of failure on the part of the mother, especially erratic behaviour, produce over-activity of the mental functioning. Here, in the overgrowth of the mental function reactive to erratic mothering, we see that there can develop an opposition between mind and the psyche-soma. (Winnicott, 1949a: 246)

The infant, of course, has no words for such an 'opposition'. If it could be put into words, we might think in terms of a phrase such as 'I am not really here' or 'It is not me that this is happening to'. In adult psychotherapy, clients do sometimes refer to experiences of opposition or disconnection between thinking and embodiment. They may speak of a sense of numbness or abstraction, of feeling that they are assessing their own words as if from a distance, of hearing words coming out of their mouths without feeling connected to the thoughts or opinions being voiced.

As with all defences, the exile of the physical and the associated dampening down of desire and emotion serve a purpose. There is no point in the infant continuing to show his true needs and wishes if they provoke reactions of hostility or disapproval, or are simply not responded to. The baby who does not feel responded to in a loving way is obliged to trade spontaneity of self-expression for a way of being that owes more to the receiving environment than to his own natural inclinations. Becoming the kind of baby his mother seems to want or need may bring some (albeit conditional) love his way. This 'false self' (Winnicott, 1960a) adaptation is at first unconscious. As the baby's mental functioning develops, he brings it into the service of a more conscious second-guessing of his mother in order to get the emotional responses that he needs. This is one version of the 'over-activity of mental functioning', to which Winnicott refers. The baby has been obliged to become prematurely calculating.

As well as, or instead of, becoming excessively compliant, a baby may respond to poor or erratic care by disavowing his vulnerability and neediness. This variety of false self-adaptation, described by Winnicott (1962) as the 'caretaker self' and Bick (1968) as 'precocious self-caretaking', has the advantage of reducing the immediate pain of the situation. At the same time, it involves the development of what Bick (1968) refers to as a toughened 'second skin'. The individual is better protected from the unbearable experience of not being loved, but his protection leaves him less permeable, less open to future relationships which may be helpful to him.

Nevertheless, Winnicott believed that a more favourable environment might eventually lead to the re-emergence of 'true self' elements, the spontaneous gesture, the unguarded expression of individual need and desire. In the meantime, these elements, which must always remain essentially private, are lost to the individual himself or herself. Many people come to psychotherapy in a crisis of indecision of one kind or another. They lack any real feeling of what they want and what they do not want. The defences that have been brought into play may also exert a more expensive toll on the individual in the form of psychosomatic illness or in feeling dissociated and unreal.

While acknowledging the enormous importance of mental development, Winnicott clearly regarded the activity of thinking with rather more suspicion than did his contemporary Wilfred Bion. Unlike Bion, Winnicott recurrently refers to the potential for mental activity to be used in a precocious and defensive manner. Bick, with whom Winnicott maintained a friendly correspondence (see Rayner, 1991), seems to have held views similar to those of Winnicott on this particular matter.

## Holding and handling

Winnicott chooses to use two terms, 'holding' and 'handling', when writing about maternal care. 'Holding' refers to the maternal activity of being receptive to the baby's communications, keeping the baby in mind and empathising with him. There are obvious similarities between Winnicott's description of 'holding' and Bion's description of 'containment' (1962), a concept which has been found to be valuable in many contexts and has been elaborated in a variety of different ways. 'Handling' refers to feeding, carrying, cuddling, kissing, dressing, changing, bathing, rocking, soothing and otherwise physically caring for the baby. Almost any infant observation demonstrates that holding and handling happen together rather than separately. They are complementary and inseparable aspects of maternal care.

Winnicott has described a young infant as 'all the time on the brink of unthinkable anxiety'. Sensing his precariousness, Winnicott's 'good enough' mother does her best to ensure that her baby's experiences are manageable:

> In the ordinary course of events the mother tries not to introduce complications beyond those which the infant can understand and allow for; in particular she tries to insulate her baby from coincidences and from other phenomena that must be beyond the infant's ability to comprehend. (1949a: 245)

In 1962, Winnicott named four varieties of 'unthinkable anxiety': 'going to pieces', 'falling for ever', 'having no relationship to the body' and 'having no orientation'. These phrases refer to the disintegration of the psyche and Winnicott himself refers to them as 'the stuff of psychotic anxieties'. Winnicott's use of physical metaphors reflects the inherent difficulty of putting words to such experiences. Essentially, they are beyond thinking. Young babies, with their very limited capacity for thinking and making sense of their experiences, are particularly vulnerable to such extreme anxieties and to a somatic expression of their distress.

Even in the best of situations, a baby will from time to time be overwhelmed by distress. He will encounter experiences that he cannot manage by himself. Through holding and handling, the mother helps the baby to recover his sense of continuity, of 'going on being', when it has been temporarily disrupted:

> With a relative absence of reactions to impingements, the infant's body functions give a good basis for the building up of a body ego. In this way the keel is laid down for future mental health. (Winnicott, 1963: 86)

On the other hand, where impingements are too frequent or too severe, the baby experiences trauma, an absolute break between before and after. In this situation, psychosomatic splitting is one of the defences likely to be brought into play, with negative consequences for psychosomatic health.

## 'Good enough' mothering

Through his work as a paediatrician and child psychoanalyst, Winnicott met with many mothers and babies. He saw that care was seldom perfect but that most failures were relatively minor and could be recovered from quite quickly. Winnicott was a great champion of the 'good enough' rather than the perfect mother. He encouraged mothers to be guided by their own feelings, thoughts and intuitions in deciding how best to care for their babies. He saw no valid place for a childcare 'expert' except where a family was running into particular difficulties. Winnicott's argument was that the 'ordinary devoted mother' knew what her baby needed, having entered into a particularly receptive state of mind that normally evolves during pregnancy and continues through the early months of motherhood. In this state of mind (see 'primary maternal preoccupation' below), most mothers accurately sense the needs and desires of their babies.

My observations of 'Jack' and 'Emma' show that 'good enough' can cover quite a range of different environments. The situation is made more complicated by the fact that what is good enough for one child may not be good enough for another. Infants vary considerably in their reactivity, their robustness and their resilience. Even within the same family, where a mother's internal resources are only just adequate – whether because of personal difficulties, depression or particularly stressful external circumstances – one infant may flourish while the development of another is adversely affected.

Naturally, this is not to deny that some circumstances are so far removed from 'good enough' that *any and every child would be traumatised by them*. At this point, constitutional differences in sensitivity, reactivity and resilience will play less of a role in the outcome. Infants who are cruelly treated, abused or grossly neglected have no choice but to activate extreme defences in order to survive:

> If the experience is too sudden, too overwhelming, the baby cannot cope and will tend to react by cutting it off, at the same time cutting off the capacity to see and to feel it. We all tend to do this temporarily with events that cause overmuch anxiety. (Harris, 1978: 12)

Winnicott described this 'cutting off' in terms of an unnatural split between psyche and soma. The traumatised infant's necessary over-reliance on such defences sets the scene for a whole range of personal difficulties in later childhood and in adult life.

## Primary maternal preoccupation

I referred earlier to the work of the intersubjectivists, describing a 'dance of reciprocity' between mother and baby. This 'dance' can be seen in some of its many forms in the interactions between Jack and his mother, and later between Emma and her mother, described below.

The evolution of these patterns depends initially on the mother's ability to interpret and respond to infant communications, some of which an outside observer would be unlikely even to notice. What is it that enables a mother to enjoy this almost magical sense of her baby's inner world? Winnicott proposes a particular emotional state, described as 'primary maternal preoccupation', in which the mother's own needs and concerns are temporarily relegated to a secondary position. Through her close identification with the baby, the 'good enough' mother senses when he needs to be fed, picked up, carried around, rocked, firmly held, loosely held or laid down and encouraged to kick and explore.

Primary maternal preoccupation permits the infant, in the very early stages of life, to maintain an illusion of omnipotence. For example, when he is hungry and the breast appears, he feels that he has in fact *created* the breast. When his mother comes and picks him up, he ideally feels that he has brought about this welcome event himself. In favourable circumstances, the mother anticipates the baby's needs and manages external events in a way that keeps their impact upon him within manageable bounds. *The infant is not aware of external care as such but simply of a continuity of going-on-being within his own body.* Through such experiences, the integrity of the psyche-soma becomes firmly grounded.

> The mother's capacity to respond to her baby's experience seems to be felt by the baby at first as a gathering together of his bodily sensations, engendering the beginnings of a sense of bodily integrity. (Miller et al., 1989: 32)

In Winnicott's scenario, primary maternal preoccupation is characteristic of the first few weeks of life, when the infant's dependency is almost total. In normal circumstances, it is a state of mind that begins to diminish quite quickly as the process described by Winnicott as 'graduated adaptive failure' comes into play. As the infant becomes able to do a little more for himself and to signal his needs more effectively, it is important that the mother does not respond prematurely and pre-empt his efforts. Where graduated adaptive failure is well paced, its timing being tailored to the needs and abilities of the particular infant in question, it supports maturation. If it is too slow, insufficient space will be made for the infant's development of his own capacity to think. If it is too fast, on the other hand, the infant is at risk of being overwhelmed by incomprehensible and unmanageable experiences. In this situation, the defence of psychosomatic splitting may be brought into play as a desperate but necessary aid to psychic survival.

# CHAPTER 7

# Touch and Well-being in Infancy

> Psycho-somatic existence is an achievement, and although its basis is an inherited growth tendency, it cannot become a fact without the active participation of a human being who is holding and handling the baby. (Winnicott, 1988: 12)

*The aim of this chapter is to consider the relationship between experiences of responsive touch and health. I will focus on observational material relating primarily to touch in this chapter and on material relating to movement in the next. Touch and movement are almost always close companions. Where handling is 'good enough', one is seldom to be seen without the other.*

## The selection of observation extracts

An observation is a microcosm of the life of baby and mother (and sometimes father, brother, sister, granny and so on) as it is lived on a day-to-day basis. As such, it captures the many different themes that are being played out simultaneously and which cannot be separated from each other in any meaningful way. In keeping with my main theme, I have selected for discussion the aspects of mother–baby interaction that have a marked physical dimension. I know, however, that the reader's attention will be caught by many other aspects of the scene observed. Although I do not have the space to discuss the many different aspects of the observations here, I hope that they will be appreciated and enjoyed.

# Early feeding experiences (Jack, Emma, Freddy)

The first three observation extracts to be presented describe three rather different feeding scenarios. Each observation involves an infant only a few weeks old. Two of the infants, 'Jack' and 'Emma', whom I observed myself, also feature in later observations. The third infant, 'Freddie', has been described in the psychoanalytic literature (Reid, 1997). The observation of Freddie is included to give a picture of a truly damaging situation, one considerably more difficult (thankfully) than those I have had occasion to observe myself.

Jack is a baby who has been cuddled and carried around a great deal from the time he was born. He is a second child, and his mother is very relaxed with him. Jack seems to have no particular difficulties in feeding or sleeping. His mother tells me cheerfully that he sleeps in bed with her and her husband. The general feeling, both from her comments and from the observations, is that she enjoys caring for Jack and takes pleasure in her tactile contact with him.

## Extract from observation of Jack at 8 weeks

Jenny opens the door carrying Jack and talking on the telephone, which is wedged between her shoulder and chin. We go into the living room. I sit down in the armchair and Jenny places Jack in my lap facing outwards, and sits down on the sofa. She smiles and gesticulates to Jack as she finishes off her telephone conversation. Jack relaxes back against me, kicking his legs and moving his hands in front of his face. He finds his right fist with his mouth and sucks it noisily. His eyes are wide open, and he watches Jenny over on the sofa.

Jenny hangs up and says to Jack, 'It's time for a feed, isn't it? You've been very patient.' She lifts up her T-shirt and undoes the zipper of her bra. Jack waves his arms and kicks his legs excitedly. He raises his head and leans his body forwards towards Jenny. Jenny comes and takes him, then settles back against the side of the sofa and swings her legs up.

Jenny says, 'Shall I feed you?' and lies Jack down in her lap. Jack curls into her body and quickly latches on to her nipple and sucks strongly and rhythmically. His eyes are open and look very dark. His gaze seems to be fixed on the fabric of the sofa. Jenny says to me, 'I love watching him feed. I know I'll miss it when he goes on to solids.' As she speaks, Jack swivels his eyes and looks at Jenny's face rather thoughtfully, still sucking.

After a few minutes, the intensity of the sucking diminishes. Now that he is not so hungry, Jack seems to be more involved in the sensual enjoyment of the feed. He licks and sucks the nipple noisily, drops it and then finds it again. He rubs his feet together, as if enjoying the slippery feeling of his cotton socks. He looks up at his socks, which are a bright lime green. Eventually, he stops feeding, relaxes back completely and each intake of breath is accompanied by small hiccuping and squeaky sounds. His eyelids droop, and finally his eyes shut. His left hand is curled into a loose fist and resting on Jenny's breast. He folds and unfolds his hand, fingering Jenny's skin. Jenny strokes his leg gently.

A few minutes later, Jenny pulls her T-shirt down, lifts Jack onto her shoulder and pats his back. He opens his eyes, looking at the square of light at the window, and yawns. Then he sits quietly in Jenny's lap, looking rather floppy, focusing his gaze on a plant for a while, then moving it back to the window. A little later, he meets and holds my gaze. In a very affectionate and endearing gesture, he rests his head on one side against Jenny's T-shirt as he looks at me, as if to say 'This is *my* Mum'.

This feed goes very smoothly and is clearly enjoyed by both parties. It has a harmonious feel, and there is a great deal of physical affection expressed from both sides, in Jack's excited kicking, strong sucking and delicate fingering, and in Jenny's loving expression and gentle stroking of her baby's leg.

The observation also shows early examples of a 'dance of reciprocity' between mother and baby. Both Jenny and Jack are quick to read and respond to the facial expressions and body movements of the other. When Jenny speaks to Jack as he sits in my lap, he leans forward towards her. When Jack sees Jenny preparing to feed him, he gesticulates and kicks his legs. When Jenny speaks to Jack during the feed, he swivels his eyes to look at her. These interactions suggest that, as well as taking in breast milk, Jack is developing his mental functioning and his capacity for relationship:

> The experience of being physically held and emotionally contained by the mother not only gives rise to a way of physically experiencing the world which might be conveyed by such terms as 'a sense of bodily integration', 'having a skin' and 'a physical sense of self'; they also bring the

baby into intimate, if primitive, contact with mental and emotional processes within the mother. (Miller et al., 1989: 32)

Winnicott specifically links handling to the question of the 'indwelling of the psyche in the soma'. As briefly described in the Introduction, the infant's sense of indwelling has its roots in the mother's integration of her own physical and emotional experiences. This integration is communicated and instilled through coherent holding and handling, which is individually tailored to meet a particular baby's needs.

For Winnicott, this process begins before the baby is born. Some readers may have had the opportunity to watch the series of television programmes made with the involvement of the Tavistock Clinic (*Talking Cure*, BBC2, 1999). In one of these, a pregnant woman speaks about her relationship with her unborn baby:

It's like when you have a pen friend. We've been writing letters to each other for long enough now. It's time to meet face to face.

The second infant presented, Emma, is also a loved and wanted baby, the first child of a couple who have been married for some years. Unfortunately, this mother finds herself in a somewhat depressed state during Emma's first year of life. As far as I know, her post-natal depression has not been diagnosed or formally acknowledged. (As an observer, it was not my place to raise the matter for discussion or to offer advice.) I am, however, able to observe that, for various reasons, this mother receives little day-to-day emotional support. Her own mother (Emma's grandmother) calls round once during an observation, makes the right noises in Emma's direction and then goes upstairs to change for a business meeting. I notice that she calls Emma by the wrong name! Emma's maternal grandfather is deceased. Her father is starting up a new business, which is clearly very time-consuming, and his parents do not reside in England. The mother's sister is nearby but has three young children of her own. By way of an indirect acknowledgement of the difficulties, Emma's mother tells me eleven months into the observation, with obvious relief, that she is 'beginning to feel very much better'.

This mother's circumstances and state of mind aroused considerable compassion in me. She struggled to be cheerful and optimistic, beginning every observation, without exception, by telling me what a good baby Emma was and listing her new achievements.

However, within a few minutes, her liveliness faded and she sank into a rather sad, withdrawn and self-absorbed state.

## Extract from observation of Emma at 9 weeks

(Emma has been feeding for five minutes.)

Emma's eyes close and she seems to be dozing at the breast, just giving the occasional suck. Almost immediately, Mother takes her nipple out of Emma's mouth and moves Emma away from her breast. Emma lies in her lap and waves her arms towards Mother's face, while looking at her intently. She makes tiny sounds and tries to turn and lean in to her mother's body. Mother looks away from her and starts to talk to me. Emma then starts to wriggle and make grumbling sounds that soon turn into a low grizzle.

Mother turns back to her and says, 'Are you going to be awful today? You're a hungry girl today, aren't you, you monster?' She says to me, 'I feel awful today. I haven't felt so awful in a long time. I've taken some paracetamol, but I've still got a headache.' In a lower tone, she confides, 'Actually, breast-feeding makes me feel awful, kind of weird, nauseous and drained.' Turning to Emma, she says, 'You're sucking the life out of me. That's what it is!'

Emma ceases crying when Mother speaks to her, but makes a series of odd, contorted faces. Her mouth is fixed in a tense crooked line and her eyes are screwed up. Mother says, 'Would you like to go in your chair?' She puts Emma in her rocker chair near me. Emma does not protest but is inert and uncooperative. Mother finds it difficult to insert her floppy legs behind the straps of the rocker chair and Emma slumps immediately to one side. Mother disappears into the kitchen and I hear her starting to make coffee, then talking on the telephone. After a couple of minutes, Emma again starts crying in a low-key grizzly way. She is collapsed in the chair with a sideways list. Her chin sinks on to her chest and she does not look up or make eye contact with me.

Although Emma often indicates through her behaviour that she would like to be held by her mother, she is in fact put down in her rocker chair at every opportunity. In the seminar group, we speculate that her mother may well be protecting her baby from her difficult and hostile feelings by putting her down. Perhaps she feels that it is better to distance herself from Emma than to subject her to the negative feelings which might be communicated through prolonged eye contact or body-to-body contact.

At the end of a similar sequence of events, five weeks later, I record my own reactions:

When Mother leaves the room to make her telephone calls, I have to bear the full impact of Emma's unmet psychological needs, her distress and her disturbance. These are only too evident in her lack of liveliness, her slumped posture, her pallid and tired appearance and her constantly running nose. When Mother is out of the room, Emma sags down, chin on chest, and cries half-heartedly in a way which seems quiet and despairing rather than demanding. Her eyes are open but vacant and unfocused. Like Mother, she seems emotionally depleted and lacking in physical energy. It is said that some babies become quite manic and try to cheer up and 'entertain' their depressed mothers, but Emma seems rather to pick up on her mother's feelings of weariness and inadequacy and becomes somewhat depressed herself. This mood is extremely infectious and I again depart from the observation feeling tired and low in spirits.

This extract offers a more detailed picture of a slumped and resigned bodymind state, which psychoanalyst Juliet Hopkins (1990) has described. In a study involving mothers who showed an aversion to physical contact to their babies, Hopkins noted:

> These babies have been found to be no less cuddly at birth than other babies are, but by a year they neither cuddle nor cling but are carried like a sack of potatoes. (Hopkins, 1990: 464)

In her study of mothers who touch their babies very little, Hopkins (1990) encountered a less extreme situation than that witnessed by Spitz (1945). The babies she observed did not die, but, as with Emma, there was a sense of them having become a 'dead weight'. Hopkins' work, like my own, suggests that an infant's whole way of inhabiting his body is an eloquent reflection of the handling he has experienced. Experiences of responsive touch, or of its absence, become visibly inscribed upon the body.

The implication here may be that we are unable to hold ourselves well if we have not been well enough held, and that this will be reflected in our muscle tone and posture. The emotional and physical aspects of such a state are two sides of the same coin, with the collapsed and sagging posture described by Hopkins encapsulating feelings of hopelessness, passivity and depression.

I have referred briefly to Bick's (1968) account of 'second skin' phenomena, which arise when a baby is not well contained. Rather than a toughened second skin to hold the infant together, albeit at the expense of permeability and a possibility of relationship, Emma seems to express a weakened sense of skin, barely any skin at all. Briggs (1997) refers to this as a 'porous skin'. Instead of manic activity and over-developed physicality, I witness a sagging posture, half-hearted crying and a lack of physical vigour. Emma's physical state seems to mimic the mother's sense of a sagging and depleted breast, which she feels to have been 'sucked dry' by her infant.

Winnicott emphasises that good enough handling supports the establishment of psychosomatic indwelling, which I have identified as being crucial to a sense of wholeness or health. If this point of view is accepted, we would expect the infant who is not well handled to have difficulty in feeling at ease within himself, at home within his skin. This difficulty may become visible in a number of ways, perhaps in a succession of psychosomatic illnesses, perhaps (as with Emma) in a slumped posture and a lack of vitality, perhaps in precocious mental development, the baby or child taking on the air of a 'little professor'.

Another possibility, poignantly illustrated in the case of Freddy, involves a visibly awkward and uneasy sense of embodiment. Freddy is an infant described by Sue Reid in a paper published in the *British Journal of Psychotherapy*. Reid describes how, during one of the observer's earliest visits, Freddy is handed to the observer. The observer notes that:

> He is a calm baby who quickly moulds himself into the shape of my body. (Reid, 1997: 552)

Unfortunately, this benign state of affairs seems destined not to last. Freddy is fed from the start:

> on the edge of the mother's knees, back towards her, with the bottle held out in front of him, so that he could not see his mother at all. (Reid, 1997: 551)

The observer senses Freddy's discomfort. This baby is not securely held but looks as if he might easily fall off the edge of his mother's lap. Throughout the feed, his mother looks towards and chats to a visitor. Freddy seems completely dropped from her mind as well as being in danger of falling physically. These inadequate experiences of holding and handling are followed in later observations by events that are felt by the observer to be actively cruel. By the time he is ten days old, Freddy is being left lying on the dining-room table on a thin blanket. Mother is usually holding her daughter Frances (aged 18 months) or otherwise engaged:

> Freddy struggled to roll himself up on the table and, when this failed, he tried to stick himself to the little blanket and turned his head from side to side with his mouth open until he found his hand and sucked on it for a long time. This seemed to keep him calm for some time before eventually he burst into tears, quickly becoming congested. Mother told him he was bad and Frances then smacked the baby, which amused mother. The observer reported that she had the greatest difficulty in not picking the baby up in her arms. (Reid, 1997: 552)

These very harsh experiences of handling seem to become inscribed upon Freddy physically, finding expression in a very strange posture. The top half of his body is described as 'hard and stiff', while the bottom half seems 'very floppy'. Reid suggests:

> Perhaps the stiff top of Freddy's body illustrated his attempt by the use of his musculature to hold himself together and to protect himself against attack, while the floppy bottom half might be seen to represent his abandonment, his unheld state. (Reid, 1997: 553)

Psychoanalytic infant observation offers a week-by-week experience of the inscription of early handling experiences upon the posture and physical appearance of a child. Such inscription, whether of positive or negative experiences of handling, forms a part of the early development of what I have described as the individual's 'body storyline'.

I will digress briefly to acknowledge how very harrowing the role of observer can sometimes be. The role of 'privileged guest' may involve the observer in living through experiences that are very upsetting. Obviously, if an infant were to be deemed 'at risk', some action would have to be taken. However, in every observation, the family has agreed voluntarily to take part. It would be exceptional to override the non-interventionist terms on which the observation has been set up.

In these circumstances, it is somewhat reassuring to know that there is some evidence that the simple presence of an observer, coupled with his or her willingness to witness and absorb distress, may be experienced as helpful (see Briggs, 1997). This is thought to be because the observer provides an additional layer of containment, through remaining present and holding on to his or her emotional contact with and thoughtfulness about the situation being observed.

In the example of Freddy, early handling experiences obviously fall outside the parameters of 'good enough', but Winnicott emphasises that the situation does not need to be so extreme for the quality of indwelling to be disturbed. Touch, in the simple sense of physical contact, only qualifies as 'good enough' handling *when it is responsive to the needs of a particular infant at a particular time.*

## Lunch time (Jack and Emma)

### Observation of Jack at 19 weeks

Jenny sits Jack in his high chair and brings over a dish of baby cereal. Jack grabs the spoon away from Jenny as she moves it towards his mouth. Then he puts his thumb and forefinger in his mouth and sucks on them, together with the cereal-filled bowl of the spoon. With his other hand, he grasps the side of the dish and tries to pull it away from Jenny, whimpering. Jenny hangs on to the dish and wrests the spoon away from Jack. She offers him another spoonful of food but he obstructs the spoon with the hand that is in his mouth. He rubs his right eye, getting cereal in it. The feed is not going well. Jack becomes more and more agitated and begins to cry, his face turning red.

Jenny wipes Jack's face, which makes him cry more loudly. Then she lifts him out of the high chair and carries him facing out over her shoulder. She paces up and down the kitchen, rubbing Jack's back and saying to me that Jack has really changed. 'I really don't feel he's my little baby any more. When he doesn't get what he wants he gets really cross and shouts at me.' She laughs and says to Jack, 'You do, don't you?' Then she says to him, 'Sometimes, you see, it's very difficult to actually know what you want.' Jack calms down and begins to look around.

Jenny helps Jack to recover from his distress by picking him up, pacing rhythmically, rubbing his back, and at the same time talking to him about what is going on. This is one of the many examples in the observation extracts of the joint and seamless operation of holding in mind and physical handling.

## Observation at 19 weeks (continued)

After a minute, Jenny notices Jack looking at the shiny kettle on the work surface. 'Can you see yourself? Who is that baby in the kettle?', she asks, at the same time swinging him in an arc closer to the kettle. Jack smiles. Jenny turns him away for a moment, then again swings him towards the kettle, repeating 'Who is that baby in the kettle?' in the same excited tone of voice. As this sequence is repeated, Jack joins fully in the game, laughing and squealing as he is swung towards the kettle and quietening momentarily as he is turned away from it.

This game illustrates what Stern has referred to as 'vitality contours'. Stern suggests that, except where there are difficulties in the area of attunement, 'vitality contours' – sequences of action and interaction characterised by a rising and falling tide of excitement – are a key aspect of mother–infant interaction. They continue to characterise many of the games that are played between a child and his parents, a child and his siblings or a child and his friends as he moves out of the infant phase. For example, 'hide-and-seek' with toddlers, in which the quietness of creeping up alternates with the excitement of discovery, has this same rhythm.

Winnicott has described how, in health, primary maternal preoccupation gradually diminishes over a period of a few months. This process, described as 'graduated adaptive failure' leaves space for the baby's development of his own capacities and resources. The pacing of adaptive failure is crucial. When all goes well, the infant is able to compensate for lapses in his mother's understanding of him by means of his own developing understanding and ability to anticipate events. By this stage in Jack's life, maternal preoccupation has, quite appropriately, diminished. Jenny sometimes feels frustrated because she is less able to sense intuitively exactly what it is that Jack wants. At the same time, she retains her capacity to recognise the right moment to invite Jack into the dance of interaction evident in the 'kettle game'.

## Extract from observation of Emma at 19 weeks

(Emma is being looked after together with her twin boy cousins. Both Mother and Mother's sister ('Aunt') are in the room).

Twin B has pulled Twin A's dummy out of his mouth and is proceeding to try to remove his left ear from his head, producing howls of rage and protest. Aunt is on the phone, but is forced to hang up and rush to the twins. She separates the boys and puts them in high chairs at the table in the kitchen end of the room. Emma is in her rocker chair, at the other end of the room. At first, she moves her head and eyes to follow events, and her face is animated. She calls to her mother, who is looking in a mirror and fixing her make-up, but receives no response. After a minute, she lowers her gaze and ceases to make sounds.

The scene is noisy and chaotic, the Twins now shouting out in their high chairs and banging their bottles on the table. Mother joins Aunt at the table and chats about her driving lesson, while Aunt prepares food and gives the twins their lunch. Emma seems quite forgotten and is not brought up to the table.

Emma clutches the bottom of her red T-shirt, screws it up with both hands, lifts it and pushes it into her mouth, where she sucks it for a while, producing a large wet patch. As she lets it drop from her mouth, I see that her face has fallen and her chin now rests down upon her chest. Her body is starting to lean sideways and sag in the chair and her eyes are downcast. Her mouth is slightly open and drooping at the corners. I feel terribly for her sadness and isolation. Checking my watch, I see that is now 15 minutes since anybody interacted with Emma. I find it very difficult not to reach out and touch her.

Emma's mother is not physically neglecting her baby, who is well fed, regularly changed and cleanly clothed. When Emma has her nappy changed, or is fed or bathed, she does, of course, receive some touch and handling, but Mother is too low in mood to play with Emma or to develop the kind of early 'conversation' described by Stern. In his work, Winnicott refers to the possibility of handling that is 'dead, useless and mechanical'. This description would be an over-statement in Emma's case, but Emma's handling is often devoid of animation. Being physically cared for by a depressed mother is by no means the same thing as experiencing handling that is enlivened by maternal enjoyment. The consequences of this difference are manifest in Emma's posture, quality of physical indwelling and general state of health.

Compared with other babies being observed, Emma at this stage lacks a definite 'personality', seeming flat, unanimated and apathetic. She does not express the liveliness and curiosity that are evident in other infants of a similar age. Emma often seems to be retreating into herself, holding on simply to the low monotone of her crying. Physically, she is pale and often suffers from colds. Her movements have a restricted feel and lack vigour, and she often looks a little hunched. Her experiences of handling are becoming 'inscribed' upon her physically and can be seen to be forming a part of her 'body storyline'.

In the observation seminar, we reflect on my physical longing to reach out to Emma, take her from her high chair, change her soggy T-shirt, wipe her nose and hold and carry her for more than a few passing moments. This, of course, I am not free to do within the methodological discipline of psychoanalytic infant observation. Instead, I find myself:

> having privileged access and exposure to the child's experience while being prohibited from intervention that might alter or ameliorate it. (Bridge and Miles, 1996: 15)

As with Nathan Field's physical experiences in the presence of clients, described as the embodied aspects of countertransference responses, my physically felt distress, my sense of yearning and my 'flatness' when I depart from the observation all seem to echo Emma's state of being. Along with other colleagues in the observation seminar, I recognise similar physical experiences in relation to some adult clients, many of whom eventually recount a history of difficult or missing experiences of touch. I shall return to this subject in Part III of the book.

In 1988, Lynne Murray carried out a psychoanalytically informed research project into the effects of maternal depression. Her work involved a group of depressed mothers and a control group of mothers in a normal state of health. Murray describes maternal depression as a flat, relatively unresponsive emotional state, involving a withdrawal into an inner world of numbness or emotional pain. This state of mind makes it difficult for a mother to read and interpret her baby's cues.

Murray found that some depressed mothers in her study handled their babies much less than did the mentally well control group. Others handled their babies for an equal amount of time but tended to pick them up *when they felt a need to do so* rather than when the baby gave an indication of wanting to be held. This difference was well illustrated for me by a client who came for psychotherapy. She described the anger and embarrassment she remembered feeling as a young schoolgirl when her mother suddenly scooped her up for a cuddle, regardless of the fact that she was absorbed in a game with a friend.

Murray noted that depressed mothers did not appear to enjoy handling their babies, although the maternal enjoyment of handling was a regular and visible feature of observations of mentally well mothers and their infants. She also noted that babies who were subject mostly to non-responsive handling cried more and were regarded by their mothers as being more difficult than those who received responsive handling. I am reminded here of Winnicott's belief that handling falls short of 'good enough' when care is just dutifully discharged. The mother's capacity to sense her baby's needs, including his need for handling experiences, is tied up with her enjoyment of his care.

## Falling apart and not falling apart

Bick described the first maternal function as being the provision of a psychic skin for the infant. Through physical care and feeding experiences, the mother provides the infant with experiences of being in one piece within a skin. This feeling of being held together is gradually internalised and can eventually be achieved by the infant without the mother's presence. Early attempts by infants to hold themselves together in the absence of the mother may involve fixed staring at an inanimate object or tensing of the muscles. All infants need to resort to these defences on some occasions, and it is important to their development that they are able to do so.

During one of my observations, Jenny asked me to look after Jack for ten minutes while she delivered his brother, aged five, to a friend's house nearby, as I describe below.

## Observation of Jack at 9 months

Jenny passes Jack to me and puts his bottle of milk on the living room shelf. Then she goes out into the hall, calling good-bye, and we hear Jenny and Tim go out of the front door. I carry Jack to the front window, and Jenny and Tim wave to him and call before disappearing into the car. I sit Jack down on the floor and sit next to him, chatting to him and offering him some toys. He looks around distractedly, then plays with a green plastic ring in a cursory manner. His face is rather anxious. I build a tower of rings and knock it over. Jack looks on with a passive, slightly lost expression and does not join in.

After a few minutes, Jack begins to cry a little and crawls restlessly a short distance in one direction and then in another, as if he doesn't know what to do with himself. I talk to him but he does not look at me. I pick Jack up, sit in the armchair with him on my lap and offer him his bottle. He sucks on it hard, staring determinedly ahead. He seems to have his gaze fixed on the curtains at the other end of the room. He sucks hard without stopping for nearly 5 minutes, feeling quite tense in my arms. Quite suddenly, I feel him relax. His eyelids droop and his bouts of sucking become short and intermittent. A minute later, he relaxes completely and is asleep.

A few minutes later, Jenny returns. She tells me that Jack seems able to send himself to sleep to escape from situations that are not to his liking. He has a minder, Alison, for two days a week and sleeps much more when Alison is caring for him than when Jenny herself is there. Not only does he extend his morning sleep to about three hours, but he also has a second long sleep in the afternoon, which is not a part of his normal routine at all.

Through fixing on the moving curtain and gathering himself together around the teat of his bottle and the experience of intense sucking, Jack is able to soothe himself and to feel held together in his mother's absence. This course of action serves him well. He does not fall apart, and he is eventually able to escape from the distressing situation altogether, by falling asleep.

These possibilities are part of an infant's normal repertoire of coping mechanisms. It is only when repeated failures of maternal care force an infant into an excessive reliance on such strategies that Bick's distortions of skin function are likely to come into play. These distortions are eloquently described by Bick as a kind of toughened 'second skin', which protects the infant against the terror of disintegration but leaves him less open to relating to others. Briggs has expanded on Bick's account, describing the alternative possibility of a 'porous skin', which feels too thin and fragile and does not enable the infant to feel properly held together.

## A psychosomatic crisis (Emma)

### Extract from observation of Emma at 10 months

Because of the Christmas and New Year break, I have not seen Emma for three weeks. I knock at the door and Mother appears with Emma on her hip. Emma is nestling into Mother's jumper and holding on the neck of the jumper with her left hand. She snuggles closer into Mother, as she peeps out at me with an interested expression.

In the living room, Mother plays with Emma on the sofa. Emma has a small pair of boots that rattle. Mother shows me that they also wind up, winds them up and gives them back to Emma. The boots go round and round in a walking motion. Emma chatters delightedly and holds the boots up to show me.

Meanwhile, Mother tells me that Emma was in hospital for 4 days over the New Year. I learn that Emma has an abscess, which formed a 'huge lump' under her chin. She had to have minor surgery and intravenous antibiotics. Mother says, with obvious satisfaction, that she stayed with Emma the whole time. She talks sympathetically about how difficult Emma found it to sleep in the daytime with the lights always on, of how good she was under the circumstances, of how exhausting it was for them both. What is being described to me is a series of intense experiences, fully shared by Emma and her mother.

During my absence, Emma has succumbed to what might be thought of as a psychosomatic crisis, perhaps expressing an unconscious bid for recovery. Is it a coincidence that Emma has succumbed to an ailment that calls for her mother's constant care, attention and support just at the time when her mother is recovering from her depressed state? Although we cannot be sure, we can say that Emma's crisis, coming at a most fortuitous moment, lends itself readily to such a reading. Psychoanalysts have long believed that any physical symptom can serve as a communication to the environment. Winnicott, in particular, emphasised the communicative value of physical symptoms as well as the difficulties they cause. In similar vein, a contemporary child and adolescent psychiatrist writes:

> Physical symptoms have been called a form of body language. Since children, by virtue of their developmental stage, have concrete thinking and limited vocabulary, physical symptoms may well be used to communicate distress…. An anxious or depressed child may have little choice but to develop a somatic complaint or disabling symptom to express his or her misery. (Lewis, 1991: 23)

Over the following weeks, Emma's physical appearance begins to reflect the changes in her relationship with her mother. Her nose stops running. Where she was pale, she is rosy-cheeked. Where her facial expression was flat and unanimated, it becomes expressive and ever-changing. Where she was quiet and withdrawn, she is cheeky and outgoing or sometimes angry and upset. Her listlessness has disappeared, and the sounds and movements that she makes are marked by a new vitality.

## Touch deprivation: research findings from other sources

Other kinds of psychoanalytic study, primate research and human physiology research have all contributed to our understanding of the role of responsive touch in infant health. A great deal of work focuses on the consequences of distortions or deficits in touch and handling, but some research considers the potential of enhanced touch experiences to sustain and support health and development.

In 1945 psychoanalyst René Spitz reported on the sad and shocking consequences of touch deprivation for hospitalised infants in the USA. Many of these infants failed to thrive in spite of adequate food and physical provision, and some of them died, apparently from psychogenic causes (that is, without evident physical disease or malnutrition). Partly as a result of the publication of Spitz's findings, conditions improved. The institutions he had visited changed or were disbanded, thus ceasing to exist as 'natural laboratories' for the study of touch deprivation.

Research involving intentional deprivation of touch experiences has been carried out using primates rather than human subjects, although some would say that this, too, raises troubling ethical issues. Nevertheless, such research has produced valuable evidence relating to the effects on health and functioning of touch deprivation. An example is the well-known work of psychologists Harlow and Harlow (1962). Their study involved the 'raising' of baby monkeys by inanimate mothers. Some monkeys had only a 'wire mother' with a bottle of milk attached, while others also had a 'terry-towelling mother', to which they clung most of the time. Some monkeys were raised in sibling groups, while others were raised alone. All of the monkeys suffered some impairment of their adult functioning as a result of their early experiences.

By far the most seriously disturbed group were those who had been raised alone. Having grown up without responsive touch and handling, they neglected themselves, did not groom properly and were completely inadequate as parents, often abandoning their own offspring. Among this 'reared alone' group, those monkeys who had the benefit of the 'terry-towelling mother' were somewhat less disturbed than those who only had a 'wire mother'. A substitute object to cling to, although by no means equivalent to a real monkey mother, did seem to some extent to mitigate the psychological damage. These findings are interesting in terms of Winnicott's work on transitional objects, calling to mind both the functions of such objects and their very real limitations.

## Kangaroo care and baby massage

Findings from human physiology regarding the role of touch add to the evidence that responsive physical handling is a non-negotiable need of the human infant. Results again suggest that human touch is crucially important to an infant from the very earliest moments of life.

Several studies, summarised by Tiffany Field (1995), describe the progress of premature babies who receive 'kangaroo care'. In this system of care, premature babies spend their early days in almost continuous skin-to-skin contact with the mother, living chest-to-chest inside her T-shirt instead of inside an incubator. (Of course, this option can only be offered to the mothers of babies whose basic physiological functions can be adequately stabilised.) It has been found that the mother's body temperature adjusts to keep the baby's temperature within the ideal range. If the baby's temperature falls, the mother's temperature rises. If the baby's temperature climbs too far, the mother's body temperature falls. There is growing evidence that kangaroo care babies do better than babies in incubators. They show less fluctuation in body temperature, heart rate and respiration rate. They gain weight more quickly and are ready for discharge from hospital significantly earlier than control group babies.

Kangaroo care also has psychological consequences:

> With kangaroo care, more mothers breast-feed, and mothers feel more fulfilled about their pregnancy. The parents become deeply attached to their infants, and they feel confident about caring for them, even at home. (Anderson in Field, 1995: 40)

In view of the various strands of evidence pointing to the benign effects of handling in early infancy, I find it surprising that hospital accommodation is not more frequently made available for the mother of a premature baby. Through the efforts of John Bowlby's colleagues, James and Joyce Robertson (Robertson, 1953), it has become accepted that an older child or baby benefits from his mother's continuous presence in hospital and may suffer greatly from a long separation. As a result, young children are no longer expected to stay in hospital without one of their parents staying as well.

At the same time, these very tiny and immature babies are required to manage alone, with very little maternal touch and soothing. Every technological effort is made in relation to their survival and health, but the evidence that they fare better when they have a great deal of physical contact with their mothers is not widely reflected in current hospital practice. Perhaps, because these babies may not survive, there is an unconscious denial of their full humanity and of their normal infant need for a full quota of responsive human touch and handling.

There have also been a number of research studies into the consequences of including premature babies in a programme of baby massage (see, for example, Barnard and Brazelton, 1990; Field, 1995). The benefits enjoyed by babies receiving massage echo those described above in relation to kangaroo care. That is to say that there were measurable benefits across a whole range of physiological indices, and, in addition, infants receiving massage seemed more contented and easier to soothe.

The benign effects of baby massage are not, of course, restricted to premature babies. Baby massage is a childcare practice that has long been a part of some traditions, for example the Ayurvedic tradition in India. It is beginning to grow in popularity in the UK as mothers, midwives and health visitors discover its wide range of beneficial consequences for the emotional and physical aspects of infant health and for the mother–infant relationship.

When he was 8 weeks old, Jenny began to take Jack to weekly baby massage sessions at the Active Birth Centre in London. I had the good fortune to be able to attend two of the classes as an observer. When I went in, I was greeted by the sight of about twenty mothers sitting on bean bags, forming a circle in the large and very warm room where the massage took place. Each of them had a naked baby in her lap, or lying next to her on a towel on the thick pile carpet. Each mother was given a small bowl of deliciously scented massage oil.

The teacher, Peter Walker, led the way through the massage, directing the mothers to each part of the baby's body in turn. The mothers massaged their babies, making long stroking movements with oiled hands along calves and thighs, over backs and buttocks. Under Peter's guidance, they gently stretched the baby's limbs and joints, to help to maintain the baby's wonderful flexibility. The massage schedule was very informal. From time to time, a mother would stop massaging and pick her baby up to breast-feed him.

The atmosphere in the room was one of great contentment and vibrancy. The babies became very calm and relaxed as their mothers' hands moved over their bodies. I saw the women exchange glances and smiles, conveying pride and admiration, sometimes looking almost embarrassed at their own pleasure in their beautiful naked babies.

Only one woman had difficulty in giving the massage in this warm and sensual atmosphere. Peter went over to help her, and it emerged that the baby was not her own. She was the child's nanny, sent by the mother so that the baby would have the benefit of being massaged. Once I understood the situation, I was not surprised that this woman found it so very difficult to enter into the atmosphere of the setting. It is likely that she found this degree of intimacy inappropriate to her role as nanny and her relationship to the infant. In addition, she may well have felt ambivalent about making too strong an attachment to a child who would not be in her life permanently. When I returned the second time, the nanny and baby had left the group.

The situation in the massage class offers one example of the way in which paid childcare differs from mothering. When all goes well in the relationship between the primary carer and the baby, there are elements present that fall outside the parameters of a service that can be paid for. These elements suffuse the detail of the psychoanalytic infant observations presented above. Even if I had not made it clear that the carers involved were the babies' mothers, I think readers would easily have guessed that this was the case. The kind of mothering illustrated can be carried out by a variety of other people – including an adoptive mother, a father, a grand-mother or a same-sex partner. It is not, however, characteristic of paid professional care.

Families juggling financial pressures, work demands and the childcare needs of infants and toddlers have to make difficult decisions, often without the degree of choice that would be ideal. In making these decisions, the healthy mother's strong emotional bond with the infant and her delight in the miracle of this small being, who is both her personal creation and a unique individual in his or her own right, are important factors to be taken into account. To make this statement is to echo Winnicott, who has emphasised that adequate physical care is not in itself enough to meet an infant's needs. Health is grounded in an experience of care that reflects the bond forged out of the baby's early dependency and wish to relate, as well as the mother's special love for her child:

> Part and parcel of holding is what Winnicott refers to as *handling* – the way the mother handles her infant in all the day-to-day details of maternal care. Here is included a mother's *enjoyment* of her baby, which is an expression of her love. (Abram, 1996: 187)

# CHAPTER 8

# Movement, Enjoyment and Health

The infant no sooner moves its limbs, and feels that they are moved at its will, than it begins to enjoy itself in the use of its own power. It is the love of power, or rather the pleasure of self-consciousness in the use of means, by which we obtain outward evidence of our own inward life, in relation to ourselves. (Dr George Moore (1848), cited in *London Review of Books*, 9 February 1995: 13)

*This chapter begins with a discussion of the special relationship, which can be seen from the very beginning of life, between movement and touch. Areas of overlap at both the physiological and the psychological level are considered. Where there is no physical impediment, infants progress reliably from early movements, such as kicking, to crawling and walking. The chapter goes on to consider the potential implications of these developments for the infant's evolving sense of self, his relationship with his mother and his enjoyment of health. As in the previous chapter, these matters are explored with the help of extracts from psychoanalytic infant observations.*

## The joy of movement

As noted by Dr George Moore, by D.W. Winnicott and by parents around the world, infants and young children enjoy the sensation of movement. In contrast to the reluctance to 'take exercise' sometimes experienced in adult life, a healthy infant seems naturally drawn towards physical self-expression through movement. The motivation to move comes from within. This is true from the very beginning of life. An older child sometimes seems to find it a torment not to be able to move around freely. Then we may hear that age-old maternal incantation 'Why can't you sit *still*?'

Maternal handling has many facets. The 'good enough' mother intuitively supports the secure establishment of indwelling through her response to and encouragement of the infant's growing physical competence. This response involves an awareness of the infant's changing state, so that, for example, being laid down to kick freely is an opportunity offered when the infant is ready to take it. It also involves the recognition of and responsiveness to the *feeling* conveyed by the movement, whether it is excited or sleepy or 'hard work', requiring concentration and effort.

In the previous chapter, I emphasised the role of handling in helping the infant to feel all in one piece within his skin. The movement involved in handling assists in infant development in other ways as well. Increasingly, the infant plays his own part in handling, making small movements in the form of postural adjustments, through which he contributes to the whole '*Gestalt*' of being picked up, being carried or being fed. The mother also helps to keep an infant's more vigorous movements within safe bounds, doing her best to ensure that he does not hurt himself when kicking out or making his first attempts to walk. This particular role continues well beyond infancy:

A friend of mine was invited into her child's classroom on Mother's Day. Each six year old was invited to say something about his or her mother. When his turn came, her son said, 'I love my Mummy because she lets me climb on the shed.' This statement of affection seemed to be informed by a love of climbing, a degree of wishful thinking and an implicit plea for the permanent presence of the mother who did not restrict the boy's activities. In fact, the mother discouraged climbing on the shed and often prohibited it. Once in a while, however, a blind eye would be turned.

Movement begins in the womb and brings the unborn baby's skin into contact with the walls of his first home. This is itself a changing experience, as the foetus grows and becomes more confined and restricted with the approach of the day of birth. Early infant care is characterised by its physicality. Feeding, being carried, being bathed, being rocked, being undressed, changed and dressed again all have a strong physical element and make up the major proportion of the baby's early experience. In health, these activities embody the mother's receptivity to and holding in mind of her infant's emotional needs. Sights, sounds and smells are present along with movement and touch experiences. However, I shall go on to argue that there is a special affinity between experiences of movement and touch.

Individual differences with regard to vigour and style of movement can be observed from birth onwards. Judy Shuttleworth has commented that:

> Some infants seem able to cry and kick out when distressed in a way which enables them to rid themselves of what is troubling them, making it possible to accept comfort at the breast. Other babies seem to cry in a more constricted way as if their misery remains locked inside them, leaving them less free to accept their mother's attention. (Miller et al., 1989: 43)

Even the earliest infant movements, such as kicking, are affected by a context of relatedness. T. Berry Brazelton has captured on video the ways in which an infant's movements are transformed by human contact. When a baby is watching and making movements toward a toy or other inanimate object, the movements are relatively jerky and uncoordinated. When a human being approaches and speaks, or makes physical contact, the baby's movements become smooth, rhythmic and circular (Brazelton, 1975).

Over time, movement activities help the infant to acquire the strength and muscularity that will eventually enable him to sit up unaided, crawl, walk, run and jump. Alongside an increase in strength, there is a progression from gross and approximate movements to precise and well-timed ones. In normal circumstances, the child's pleasurable and expressive use of the body is accompanied by a growth of competence and confidence. Experiences of movement activities, and of the particular way in which movements are received and responded to, become a part of each person's individual body storyline.

Early experiences of movement have been the subject of less research and less thought than early experiences of touch. Nevertheless, I believe that touch and movement are both vital, and in many ways inseparable, aspects of handling in infancy and eventually of what we might think of as 'self-handling' in adult life.

## Movement, touch and proprioception (Jack)

As well as describing and considering the significance of maternal handling, Winnicott proposed a kind of *innate push towards using the body*, which is supported by the physicality of the mother–infant relationship. This push is in the service of a general tendency towards growth and development, which remains active into and through adult life:

> The central self could be said to be the inherited potential which is experiencing a continuity of being, and acquiring in its own way and at its own speed a personal psychic reality and a personal body scheme. (Winnicott, 1960b: 46)

We know from the work of the intersubjectivists that all the senses operate in a cross-modal and coordinated way almost from the moment of birth. Over and above this, it seems to me that touch and movement experiences have a particular connection to each another. This argument is based on a consideration of the *physiological* processes involved jointly in both movement and touch, as well as of the *experiential* overlaps of touch and movement, which can be freely observed in everyday life.

The physiological affinity between touch and movement comes from the involvement in both of the same nerve receptors, located in the muscle layer and at the surface of the skin. Movement stretches the skin and brings the surface receptors into play. The pressure of touch is felt in the muscle layer below the skin and activates the receptors also involved in physical activity and in the operation of proprioception, the 'positional sense' referred to earlier.

As we have seen, there is considerable evidence that inadequate handling is reflected in poor posture and developmental delay. Posture involves subtle movements whereby the infant makes small bodily adjustments on the basis of proprioceptive feedback. Where the baby is well handled from the start, he seems to learn quite quickly to hold himself together with his muscles, maintaining a posture that is toned but not rigid.

There is a parallel here with the process of containment described by Bion. In containment, the mother's holding in mind of the infant and her activity of thinking about and making sense of his experiences offers a basis for the infant's internalisation of

the thinking function. In handling, the mother's respectful attention to the baby's physical needs offers a basis for the internalisation of self-handling and self-care. We see this first in the infant's
posture and active participation in handling events. Poor handling
offers no basis for this process 'of internalisation and is reflected in
either a rigid posture, a sagging posture, or perhaps a combination
of the two, as was seen in the case of Freddy.

## Observation of Jack at 8 weeks

Mother is walking around the room, holding Jack in the crook of her left arm.
She leans right down to pick up one of his toys off the floor. Jack adjusts
perfectly to her posture, keeping himself parallel to Mother's body as she
bends over and then returns to an upright position.

But for his own postural adjustments, Jack would have fallen into
an upside-down position when his mother bent over. He has been
participating in his handling since he was born, for example by
moulding into his mother's body when she first picked him up. By
the age of eight weeks, he has expanded his repertoire. He is able
to keep his body lined up with his mother's even when she bends
right over.

Winnicott emphasises the importance of the mother's recognition of and respect for the baby's active participation in all kinds of
experience. In relation to feeding, he writes that:

> it is not so much a question of giving the baby satisfaction as of letting
> the baby find and come to terms with the object (breast, bottle, milk,
> etc.). (1962: 59–60)

Similarly, the baby needs to 'find and come to terms with' being
picked up, set down and carried, and to be accorded a space for his
or her active participation in these handling events. When all goes
well, as with Jack in the example above, infants are active in being
held and carried. The demands made upon them are in line with
their developing capacities, their postural and positional changes
forming a part of the activity.

Joan Blackmer Dexter, mentioned in Chapter 5, is one of the
few psychoanalytic psychotherapists to have referred specifically to

proprioception. Her interest derives in part from her previous career as a dancer and teacher of dance. Blackmer Dexter refers to proprioception as an 'inner tactile sense', and this is the way in which it is understood here. What I propose is that maternal handling first gives the infant a sense of the body and its limits from the outside. Very quickly, this experience becomes connected with internal sensations through the operation of proprioception. Through this conjunction, the scene is set for a good quality of indwelling, for a full and physically based experience of self as separate and yet connected.

## Early infant play (Jack and Emma)

### Observation of Jack at 9 weeks

I arrive and am shown into the kitchen. Jenny asks me if I will hold Jack while she makes a cup of tea. Jack is very lively in my arms. He is breathing quite rapidly and noisily and constantly moving his arms and legs. Jenny says, 'He's like this most of the time – always on the go!'

The tea arrives and Jenny takes Jack and puts him in his rocker chair. He gives her a big smile and she chats to him, telling him she is going to get his nappies from upstairs. When she leaves the room, Jack is alert in his chair. He becomes more still and looks all around with an interested expression.

Jenny returns and goes over to Jack. Again, he gives her a big smile. She crouches down and tickles him and he bursts into huge smiles and giggles. She lifts him out of his chair and we go into the living room. Here, Jenny lays Jack on his changing mat and gently undresses him. Before she removes his nappy, Jenny puts Jack's arms inside another babygro so that he doesn't get cold, saying, 'There. That's a nice fleecy one for you. You'll like that one.' She removes Jack's nappy and tells me he has nappy rash and that she will leave it to 'air' for a bit.

Jack seems to like the freedom of lying with bare legs on the mat. He stretches his legs right out, bends them up one at a time, then kicks them out again and points his toes. He moves the sole of one bare foot over the top of the other in a stroking movement, all the time watching his feet. He turns his head and upper body right over in one direction and then back in the other, kicking his legs and moving his arms with great animation. He catches sight of me watching him, becomes still and holds my gaze, looking at me intently for about half a minute.

Tim (aged 5) comes into the room, comes over to me and asks me what I am doing. He takes no notice of Jack and, at this stage, Jack takes no notice of him. When Tim goes out, Jenny tells me that he is off school because of an 'accident' yesterday, when he had diarrhoea at school. I ask Jenny if Tim was upset by this, and she tells me that Tim in fact denied that it had happened to him at all, saying, 'It was the baby that did it.'

Jenny goes over to Jack, still lying on the mat, looking around and moving his limbs. She rubs his tummy and says 'What a big tummy. That's my milk in there.' She looks at me and says, 'Isn't he lovely, though?' I agree that he is. Then she puts his new nappy on, dresses him carefully, picks him up and we return to the kitchen. Jenny puts Jack in his rocker chair again and moves around the kitchen, tidying up. Jack's eyes follow her moves all around the kitchen.

Tim comes in and needs all Jenny's attention. He wants to take some vitamins, and there is a form that has to be filled in for school. After a while, Jack starts to make grumpy noises and then to cry. Jenny lifts him out of the chair and talks to him. After a minute, she asks if I will hold him, hands him to me and leaves the room with Tim. Jack feels very soft as he sits on my lap and moulds himself to my body. I turn him to face me and he gazes at my face very calmly, breathing easily. After a minute, he lifts up one hand and touches my cheek.

Jenny returns and asks Jack if he is hungry. As she lifts him off my knee, he becomes more excited and seems to know that he is about to be fed. He butts gently against Jenny's breast and his eyes look dark and shiny. It is time for me to leave, and I say my goodbyes as Jenny takes Jack into the living room to feed him.

This observation reveals play as an activity which essentially involves movement and touch. In its earliest form, it is centred around the infant's exploration of his own and his mother's body. During the observation hour, Jack has the opportunity to compare experiences of being touched by Jenny with experiences of touching his own body and touching my face. Through touching his own body, he has the experience both of touching and of being touched.

William Hoffer (1950) suggested that such 'double touch' experiences have a particular role in infancy, helping to establish a sense of skin, a sense of 'me' and 'not me'. They help the baby to work out what is within his own body and what lies in the outside world:

> Coming in touch with its body elicits two sensations of the same quality and these lead to the distinction between the self and the not-self, between the body and what subsequently becomes the environment. (Hoffer, 1950: 19)

In Winnicott's terms, we might say that Jack is taking lessons in:

> the perpetual *human* task of keeping inner and outer reality separate yet interrelated. (Winnicott, 1953: 230)

## Observation of Emma at 9 weeks

I knock at the door and Aunt lets me in. Mother is breast-feeding Emma in the living room. Emma is sucking strongly, her body still and relaxed. As usual, Mother begins by telling me how wonderful Emma is. 'She's so good! She only woke me once in the night last night and she hardly every cries, except when I'm changing her nappy.' While Mother speaks, Emma rests one hand gently on her breast. Her dark eyes are turned upwards, gazing at mother's face.

Mother begins to talk to Emma in a teasing kind of way. 'You've got such beady eyes, haven't you. But you look such a sweet girl when they're closed.' Emma starts making gulping noises and Mother takes her off the breast. 'You can't take it all in at once. Now look what a mess you've got yourself into.'

Mother sits Emma up on her knee and says 'Can you do a burp?' Emma obliges and Mother tells me that she often doesn't burp and that she then 'sicks up' her milk later. Mother lays Emma down on her lap. Emma constantly moves her arms and legs and continues to move her mouth as if she is still feeding. She looks rather uncomfortable and unsupported. I can see that she looks intently at Mother whenever she speaks. I say, 'She really looks at you now when you are talking.' Mother says, 'I think *maybe* she can see. I'm not sure if she can focus yet... .' Emma grimaces and then gives a crooked smile. Mother says, 'I know she can't really smile yet, but when that smile crosses her face when she's sleeping, it's so sweet. I do hope her smile will be like that when it's a proper smile. It's such a lovely smile for a little girl.'

At the beginning of the observation, Emma shows her enjoyment of feeding and of being held, sucking contentedly and touching her mother's breast. But Emma's dependency seems to stir up very difficult feelings, perhaps related to the mother's own experiences as a baby (see Raphael-Leff, 1984). Mother experiences baby Emma as beady-eyed, messy and voracious, and daydreams about a time when she will have a 'little girl' with a 'proper smile'. At one point, I share one of my observations with the mother, pointing out that that Emma recognises and responds to her. This is one of the ways in which an observer may be able to be helpful in a difficult situation without stepping too far outside the observer role.

## Observation of Emma at 9 weeks (continued)

Mother says to Emma, 'Would you like to play with your Babygym?' She puts Emma in her rocker chair and puts the Babygym over it, so that the suspended toys are within Emma's reach. Mother leaves the room to make a phone call and Emma slumps in her chair, taking no interest in the toys. Soon she begins to cry in a low key way. Eventually, Mother finishes her phone call and returns.

Mother crouches down by the chair and says to Emma apologetically, 'I just don't feel up to playing with you today. I know it's a bit mean.' When Mother speaks, Emma stops crying and looks up, but her expression is dull and vacant. Mother makes what seems to be a huge effort, talking about an orange plastic chicken on the Babygym and jiggling it for Emma. Emma yawns, looks at the toy, then looks back towards Mother's face and whimpers a little.

Mother moves away and collapses wearily in the armchair, looking at Emma with a defeated expression. She says, 'Let's change your nappy then.' She does not move, and both Emma and Mother sag in their chairs, half dozing. Five minutes later, Mother says again, 'Come on then. Shall we get you out and change you?', but still does not move. Emma again begins to cry.

Mother feels too drained and low in spirits to engage in reciprocal play with Emma. In the face of these difficulties, she makes an effort to substitute toys for herself. At this early stage, however, the toys hold no interest for Emma except in so far as Mother is able to bring them to life and inject some excitement into them. This is also beyond Mother's current capacities, and the interaction fizzles out, leaving all three of us feeling weary and inert. The situation becomes oppressively static. All three of us have ground to a halt.

Readers will know from an observation in the previous chapter that Emma is sometimes cared for jointly with her twin cousins, who are three months older than her. Her mother weans her from the breast at four months (which Emma finds enormously distressing), and at this point a more regular system of childcare 'shifts' involving all three children is inaugurated. Mother tells me that Emma needs other children to play with and that she 'loves being with the boys'.

## Observation of Emma at 17 weeks

(We are in Aunt's living room. Emma has been propped into the corner of the sofa, but has toppled over and is now lying down.)

Twin A crawls over to Emma, pulls himself up on the sofa and pats her body. Emma smiles and kicks. Twin A reaches for her face, feeling it with his hand. Emma responds by gently stretching her hand towards him and touching his face in return. Twin A again feels Emma's face, this time too hard, squashing her nose and brushing her eye with one of his fingers.

Emma's face crumples and she begins to cry. As Mother has left the room and Aunt is busy with Twin B, I rescue her by picking her up.

Mother wants to be able to offer Emma something good. Faced with her own weariness and depletion, she seems to idealise the extended family setting. In one way, the change of scene *is* good for Emma, and she clearly enjoys the liveliness and movement around her. When she is safely in a high chair, she sits watching the boys' antics and becomes much more animated. And, as in the above extract, she shows that she wants to play, and she tries to join in.

Because she is younger, smaller and more vulnerable, however, Emma needs individual support and protection. She cannot play with bigger boys, three months older and already mobile, without frequently getting hurt. Aunt has her hands full with the twins, and Mother is often emotionally absent, even when she is in the room.

The situation has a way of pulling me in and on many occasions, I am the one to 'rescue' Emma.

On one occasion I am invited to see Emma in the bath with the two boys; Mother tells me that 'they love to have a bath together'. The situation I witness strikes me as frightening and overwhelming for Emma. The boys are very excited. They stand up and laugh and stamp in the water. Being smaller and less physically competent, Emma is bumped and splashed until she eventually cries miserably and has to be taken out of the bath. Mother says to me, 'I'm afraid she's a bit of a wimp.' On all of these occasions, it seems that Emma is being regarded as older and more competent than she actually is. In her mother's mind, she is perhaps already the 'little girl' whom she feels she could look after well, rather than the dependent baby who is actually in the room.

> Observers may notice a marked difference between what mothers say about their babies and what seems to be in reality true of them. (Bridge and Miles, 1996: 15)

## Movement and psychosomatic recovery (Emma)

The close association of movement and touch continues as a child gets older. We have all seen children crawl, walk or run towards a person with whom they want to make physical contact. A child may take matters into his own hands, perhaps climbing on to a knee or wrapping his arms around a leg. Or he may signal his wish to be touched in a variety of ways, stretching out his arms in an unmistakable plea to be picked up or asking in words to be carried. His self-propelled movement brings about proximity, and proximity sets the scene for the touch experiences that follow.

Neither is this close association between touch and movement lost in adult life. The young man waiting on the station platform sees his lover waving from the window of the train. As she alights, he runs towards her. The movement, the approach, moves seamlessly into the passionate embrace which follows.

Esther Bick and her colleagues have described how, in adverse circumstances, a young child may use mobility in a negative way, as a 'second skin' defence against dependency. This defence is sometimes associated with a marked degree of hyperactivity. The child may be physically rough with other children and seem impervious to the needs and wishes of others. This is, of course, a serious situation, with negative implications for the child's future relationships and emotional development. This 'toughened second skin' scenario is well illustrated in the film, made by James and Joyce Robertson in the 1950s, of 'John', a two-year-old child who is placed in a nursery while his mother is in hospital giving birth to her second child. John is a family child who has been well cared for and is sensitive to the needs of others. Among the 'tough' children who have grown up in an institution, he is unable to compete successfully either for toys or for adult attention, eventually becoming withdrawn and depressed.

Where an infant has been well held and handled, the development and use of mobility is likely to evolve in an emotionally healthy way, coming into the service of relatedness rather than of self-sufficiency. I have not to date come across many examples of this 'healthy' scenario in print and I am pleased to be able to offer some here. Another possibility, also illustrated below, involves the potential for mobility to operate in the service of recovery. For Emma, who certainly experienced early deficits of handling but who was nevertheless a loved child, mobility seems to have offered a second opportunity to establish a good relationship with her mother.

In any individual case, a great deal depends on the severity of the damage already suffered and on the way in which the infant's growing physical competence is experienced and received by the mother. Prior to becoming mobile, infants have been employing a repertoire of ways of signalling their wishes for contact and communication. Whether these signals receive an appropriate response depends upon the mental health as well as the normal sensitivity of the mother. The depressed mother usually has good intentions but is not in a state of mind to pick up on these signals.

In my observation of Emma, I was fortunate enough to witness her extraordinary resilience and capacity for recovery. Towards the end of her first year of life, a substantial change occurred. As described in the previous chapter, Emma had a stay in hospital with her mother shortly after her first birthday. This roughly coincided with other changes both within and around Emma. Of great significance was the lifting of her mother's depressed mood, a change which had begun a few months earlier. Indirectly acknowledging her previous depression, Emma's mother told me with relief that she was feeling much better. In the meantime, Emma had learned to crawl and was shortly to begin walking. During the observation it began to seem to me that becoming mobile might have a particular importance for infants whose mothers have suffered from maternal depression. With the achievement of independent locomotion, a new range of possibilities comes into play. Now, Emma did not need to rely so much on her mother tuning in to her cues. She could act on her wishes in a more direct way, approaching, moving away and initiating direct physical contact with her mother.

The combination of these developments brought to an end the passivity, the sense of helplessness and abandonment, that had become so characteristic of Emma She began to act more decisively and effectively on her own account. In addition, these changes in Emma seemed in turn to reassure her mother that no lasting damage had been done. Emma was able to show quite clearly that, in spite of the difficulties in their relationship, she had preserved her mother as a 'good object' (Klein, 1946, 1957). Her new-found mobility made it easier for her to show her love.

## Observation of Emma at 11 months

Mother and Emma are in the living room. Emma is crawling around the room, while Mother sits on the large and well-padded sofa, reading the newspaper.

Emma's first stop is at a picnic hamper, lying with its lid open on the floor. With difficulty, she climbs inside it, wriggling and curling herself to sit in the confined space. When she is settled, she looks over at Mother with great self-satisfaction, pursing her lips and making happy talking sounds. Mother laughs. 'You are funny', she says. Immediately, Emma climbs out of the basket, crawls over to Mother and pulls herself into an upright position, using Mother's leg for support.

Emma tries to climb up – it is quite high. After several attempts, she gets a knee up onto the cushion and manages to lever herself up, then pulls herself into a standing position next to Mother, this time using the back of the sofa to help her. Mother is still trying to read the newspaper. Emma chats to her, 'Uh-uh. Yeah-yeah', then throws herself front down over Mother's knee, scrunching the newspaper and giggling. Mother puts her arms around Emma and laughs. 'You'll fall off the sofa!', she says jokingly. She sets the crumpled newspaper aside. Smiling and happy, Emma crawls around the sofa and around Mother's lap, burying her head in the soft cushions and then in Mother's skirt and croaking softly. She pulls herself up and again flings herself face down over Mother's knees in delightful abandonment, relying on Mother not to let her fall off. Mother cuddles her and tickles her, saying, 'You'll fall, you'll fall!' but not really sounding at all worried. Emma again crawls all around the sofa, head down, butting, snuggling and snuffling like a little animal on all fours. Then she again pulls herself up using the back of the sofa and throws herself onto Mother. This sequence of Emma standing momentarily, then throwing herself down, is repeated many times. Each time it becomes a little more daring and abandoned. The game is accompanied by high-pitched squeaks of excited laughter. Eventually Emma approaches the edge of the sofa and looks over. 'Go off backwards', warns Mother, and helps her down.

Emma seems to greatly enjoy her new-found mobility, and it may be that crawling and walking, in themselves, help to compensate for her earlier paucity of touch experiences. Perhaps more importantly, mobility enables her to elicit from her mother experiences of touch and handling that had been lacking in earlier months. As well as illustrating the growing enjoyment of handling on the part of both mother and infant, this extract illustrates the points made about the experiential overlaps of movement and touch. Emma approaches, climbs, snuggles, is cuddled, is tickled, and all of this forms a part of a cohesive experiential whole.

A month later, Emma has apparently internalised the experience of good handling to a degree that enables her to 'hold on' for a little while when she cannot gain physical proximity to her mother.

## Observation of Emma at 12 months

Mother heads for the stairs and Emma immediately leaves her toy and crawls to the wooden gate, crying. Mother talks to her in a patient and comforting tone. 'It's all right. I'm here. I'm just going to the kitchen to put the kettle on'. Emma is appeased and returns to her keyboard. She resumes her thoughtful, deliberate, one-finger playing of the notes. She looks at me, makes chattering, word-like sounds and then turns back. She presses a coloured button that starts a drum rhythm, then becomes very excited and starts hitting bunches of keys together with her two hands. She becomes distracted by some lively music coming from the radio and crawls away from the keyboard. Holding on to the back of a chair, she pulls herself into a standing position and begins to 'dance', bobbing up and down as she bends her knees to the rhythm of the music.

Emma again approaches the gate to the stairs. She 'talks' quietly through the bars and looks longingly down the stairs. She tries to put her knee through the gap between the wooden posts, then puts her hand through and points down, turning to look at me sadly. She starts to cry. 'Don't worry, darling. I'm coming. I'm making coffee', calls Mother. Emma stops crying and clearly calls down the stairs 'Mummee!' She looks around and spots a pile of small pieces of paper on her desk. She crawls over and picks them up, then brings them back to the gate. One by one, the pieces are posted through the gaps in the gate and go fluttering down the stairs towards the sounds of Mother in the kitchen.

We hear the phone ring and Mother answer, and Emma starts to cry again. Mother comes upstairs with the phone, saying 'Look, I'm sorry. I'll have to ring you back in a minute' and then hangs up. She comes to Emma and picks her up. 'You don't like being ignored, do you?', says Mother, and then, 'It's not surprising.' She sweeps Emma up, holds her aloft, then brings her back down and blows raspberries on her neck. Emma giggles with delight. Then Mother carries Emma over to the phone and sits on a chair. As she dials a number, Emma sits happily in her lap, playing with the phone cord.

In the seminar group, we reflect on the enormous physical, intellectual and emotional strides that Emma has made within a very short space of time. She is now a lively child, quick to grasp what is going on. These changes seem to delight her mother, who is able to enjoy her daughter fully at last. Now that her mother is more available, Emma is able to tolerate short separations from her without collapsing or falling apart. These changes have also affected Emma's relationship with the observer. Whereas she was withdrawn and reluctant to make eye contact, she is now often outgoing and communicative, and is able to use the observer as a secondary resource.

How is it that Emma has been able to 'hold on' until a combination of changed circumstances has presented her with the opportunities she needs? Might it be that, at an unconscious level, each of us has and retains a sense of what it is to be properly held, even if we have not in reality had the experience of good handling? Whether or not this is the case, everyone in the group is struck by the rapid change observed in Emma, her evident vigour and energy, and her eager engagement with the environment.

Through the practice of observation, I have become far more aware of the extraordinary resilience of young children. A normal childhood is a very mixed bag, often not so much a matter of a continuous smooth ride as of a million minor recoveries. Many young children go through difficult patches. Perhaps, as with Emma, there is maternal depression. Perhaps there is bereavement in the family or a divorce. Infant observations suggest, however, that we have reason to feel hopeful for children, with the possible exception of those who are in the most adverse circumstances or whose suffering goes on for an intolerable length of time.

## Learning to walk (Jack)

In many families, learning to walk is regarded as a landmark achievement and first steps are greeted with great excitement. Unlike crawling, walking involves minimal contact with the ground, and this 'free-standing' quality gives the sense of an infant being much more his own person. The infant's experience has two aspects. On the one hand, there is the new sensation of being able to move tentatively forward on his own two feet, with all that such an achievement may mean. On the other hand, there is the way in which this achievement is greeted (or not greeted) by significant others.

Learning to walk is, as Winnicott put it, 'imaginatively elaborated' by the people close to the child as well as by the child himself. It is widely identified as a key moment in the transition from infancy to childhood. It marks the shift from being carried or wheeled around to moving independently from place to place. This shift is partially pre-figured by crawling, but crawling is not an adult form of locomotion, and we accord it a lesser significance. We intuitively recognise that its possibilities are limited. We do not, for example, imagine a child crawling to school.

What does it mean for parents to have a child who can walk? There may be relief that the child has survived the first and most vulnerable phase of his life. Perhaps there is pride that the baby is turning into a child and one can begin to see the adult he may become. Whatever unconscious processes are at work, it is evident that, in benign circumstances, this entirely normal and predictable development is often a source of wonder and celebration. A camera may be produced to record the event or telephone calls made to pass on the news to relatives and friends. The baby is quick to catch on to this atmosphere of excitement and admiration.

## Observation of Jack at 11 months

Mother opens the front door, carrying Jack in her arms. 'Maggie, you must come and look at what Jack can do. He's almost walking!' I follow her into the living room, where she sets Jack carefully down on his feet. He takes two tentative, wobbling steps over to the sofa, where he leans forward and supports himself. Jack looks up at me and gives me a broad smile. Jenny says, 'I can't believe it. Those were his first real steps.' She looks at me. 'They were real steps, weren't they?' I agree that they were. Jenny applauds Jack, clapping and saying, 'Well done, Jack!' in an excited high-pitched voice. Jack sits back on his heels and joins in the applause, clapping his hands together. He bounces up and down on his haunches, flapping his arms up and down in time with the bouncing and laughing out loud. Responding to the elated mood, I join in the applause.

(Later, in the kitchen)

Jack crawls over to me and stretches up his right hand, clearly wanting me to take it. When I do, he pulls himself on to his feet and tugs gently on my arm. I get up and we walk around the kitchen together, Jack concentrating quietly and keeping a firm hold of my hand. After a minute or two, Jack lets go and sits down gently. He looks up and says, 'Da-da-da-daa' to me and laughs. Then he crawls to his play kitchen, pulls himself up and bangs his hands down exuberantly on his toy cooker, all the time laughing and chattering to himself.

This observation was one of the most delightful that I have undertaken. When Jack placed his small hand in mine and tugged gently, I experienced a strong body memory of each of my own children's hands creeping into mine and of that particular tug on the arm, urging me to walk with them. Jack could hardly have provided a better example of mobility being used in the service of relationship.

There are, of course, as always, less happy possibilities. In a family where the mother is depressed or in an institutional setting, the achievement of walking may pass more or less unnoticed. If the mother is severely over-burdened, the infant's increased mobility may be an enormous nuisance. And in all families, there will inevitably be a change in the parents' perception of and response to their child, with a corresponding adjustment of relationships from both sides. The infant who can walk is suddenly seen as more separate, more autonomous, more his own person than the child who crawls. While this is often a cause for pride and celebration, it may also bring feelings of regret.

## Observation of Jack at 11 months (continued)

Jenny lifts Jack into his high chair and straps him in. She says to him, 'I have to do this now, don't I Jack, otherwise you'll climb out.' She says to me, 'He's really a toddler now, isn't he? And he's so much his own person, not really like a baby any more. You know, he knows what he wants. If he's strapped in and wants to get out, he roars like a lion!'

From the beginning, a person's way of walking is a very personal and individual thing, shaped by constitutional endowment, the receiving context he encounters when he takes his first steps and the handling he has received prior to becoming mobile. Like other physical activities, walking may evolve on the basis of good enough maternal care, when it remains linked to ego development and to earlier experiences of handling, or it may develop in a split-off way, expressing a toughened 'second skin' and fuelling a degree of pseudo-independence that is already excessive.

Emma moves from crawling to walking in the space of only three months. Her mother is very proud of her achievement, which seems to confirm that Emma is undamaged by her early experiences, that the present can be enjoyed and that the future can be looked forward to. Walking makes it possible for Emma to include herself in her cousin's play, with less risk of being inadvertently trodden underfoot and hurt. She gains confidence in her relationships with them and this seems linked to a general growth in confidence. She becomes much more interested in me and begins to regard me as a resource. Now, when her mother is on the telephone, she approaches me with a toy and 'chatters' to me.

Although their early experiences have been very different, both Emma and Jack seem to have received care that is 'good enough'. Both seem able to use their new-found mobility in a way that is helpful to their development and that comes into the service of relatedness and of health.

## 'Style' and 'quality' of psychosomatic indwelling

Along with other experiences of touch and movement, physical identifications become woven into a person's body storyline. They also form a part of a family likeness. We often recognise that people are from the same family because of the similarities in their posture, gestures, ways of walking, ways of running and so on.

Personal experiences interact with the wider cultural context. French people are renowned for their expansive gestures. Upper-class people walk with a certain posture and bearing. The French philosopher, Baudrillard, has referred to these aspects of embodiment as a person's 'habitas'. They are a part of what we might call the *style* of a person's indwelling. This style reflects the wider influences of an individual's culture and social position.

My particular concern here is with *quality* of indwelling, which is a more specific and personal matter, deriving from individual one-to-one experiences with significant others:

> Good-enough handling results in the infant's 'psyche indwelling in the soma'; Winnicott refers to this as 'personalization'. This means that the infant comes to feel, as a consequence of loving handling, that his body is himself or/and that his sense of self is centred in the body. (Abram, 1996: 187)

# Part III

## Adult Case Studies

# CHAPTER 9

# The Body and the Word

Every bodily process is directly or indirectly influenced by psychological stimuli because the whole organism constitutes a unit with all of its parts interconnected. (Alexander, 1950: 12)

*Part III of the book turns to the question of recovery in situations where a good enough quality of indwelling has either never been properly established or has been damaged or lost somewhere along the line. Where respectful and responsive touch experiences have been lacking in infancy, or where there has been trauma in this area of experience, what health-seeking options are open to the adult? How can the recovery of psychosomatic health best be supported in the psychotherapy setting?*

## 'Indwelling' in adult life

In his writing, Winnicott both endorses and extends the point of view expressed by Alexander above. However, his account of the interplay of verbal and bodily experiences centres on childhood 'handling' experiences. He does not specifically consider the contribution to adult well-being of what I have called 'self-handling', a term I use to refer to adult activities involving a conscious or unconscious quest for experiences of touch and movement. My consideration of the role of self-handling in underpinning a good sense of indwelling in adult life therefore involves an elaboration of Winnicott's ideas.

There are some general indications to work from. We know that Winnicott was more drawn to the Kleinian idea of 'positions' – to be revisited and grappled with many times during the course of a lifetime – than to the Freudian idea of 'stages', which could, in theory, be successfully completed and left behind for good. Klein (1946) had emphasised that the paranoid schizoid position, in which bad feelings are split off from good feelings in order to ensure the survival of the latter, would be returned to again and again at times of crisis. Winnicott intimated that a different kind of split – a split between psyche and soma – was also a recurrent risk in adult life. In 1962, he wrote that:

> Certain tendencies in personality growth are characterized by the fact that they can be discerned from the very beginning, *and they never reach completion* (my italics). (Winnicott, 1962: 69)

Among such 'tendencies in personality growth', Winnicott included:

> What might be called 'in-dwelling': the achievement of a close and easy relationship between the psyche and the body, and body functioning. (p. 69)

It is clear from these passages that Winnicott believed that there was an ongoing possibility of gain (and, by implication, of loss) in the quality of physical indwelling throughout adult life. And since he had linked quality of indwelling so closely with experiences of handling in infancy, it seems reasonable to imagine that he would have considered self-handling to be of significance in adult health.

## A confusion of tongues

> By implication, psychoanalytic interpretation, like all verbal expressions, cannot escape intimate links with the body. It is inseparable from sounds that are emitted physically, and thus from intonation, volume, rhythm and other forms of primitive enactment. (Likierman, 1993: 446)

Therapy practitioners who include touch and movement techniques in their work sometimes suggest that verbal therapies, such as psychoanalysis, ignore the physicality of the client. This is by no means the case for no psychotherapist can disregard the fact that both therapist and client are embodied beings. Much of the psychoanalytic psychotherapist's understanding of a client's psychological state comes from allowing and reflecting on the impact of the client's posture, facial expression, quality of gesture and physical style. This impact may make itself felt in the form of

a thought arising in the therapist's mind or in a more directly physical manner, for example in a headache or a feeling of discomfort
or restlessness. Working with a good awareness of somatic aspects
of the countertransference is therefore seen as being crucial to the
success of psychoanalytic psychotherapy. Recent contributions to
the literature and discussions arising from these contributions are
bringing a new focus on this subject. In June 2000, for example, a
conference entitled 'The Therapist's Body', organised by the Freud
Museum, was attended by 350 therapists.

As Likierman points out, the psychotherapist who offers a verbal
communication at the same time offers a physical communication.
The same applies to client communications. The way in which
something is said, the loud or soft tone, the play of emphasis within
the phrase, all communicate at least as much as the representational content of the words used. This becomes particularly
obvious when physical and representational aspects of a verbal
communication disagree – for example, when a person says in a
timid whisper that he is absolutely furious with his wife. Silence,
usually accompanied by a particular quality of gaze, is equally
communicative. In addition, gesture is a part of the language of the
therapist as well as of the language of the client.

In our different ways, then, we all work physically and with the
physicality of the client. There is a distinction, however, between
working in a 'hands-on' way and in a way that does not involve
direct physical contact. This distinction resides in technique, in the
form that the therapeutic practice takes. Both bodywork and verbal
approaches, if they are to be effective, must encompass a sensitivity
to non-verbal communication and to quality of indwelling. In this
sense, all psychotherapy is essentially 'holistic'.

## Listening with the body

With regard to transference and countertransference phenomena,
I have adopted as my own framework the scenario sketched out by
Thomas Ogden and summarised in Chapter 4. In this model, the
client's transference feelings towards the therapist and the therapist's countertransference feelings towards the client are thought
of as being enjoined in a matrix. As with Winnicott's 'transitional
space' between mother and baby, this matrix lies between therapist

and client and belongs to neither of them. Each party both contributes to the matrix and draws upon it in an unconscious way. Thus, it is a third element, or as Ogden describes it a 'third other', present in the consulting room.

Elements within this matrix may become available to the therapist in a number of ways – as a feeling, as an image, as a thought, as a physical sensation. When they take the form of a physical sensation, they are often referred to as examples of a 'somatic countertransference'. This phrase has been used in both psychoanalytic and bodywork psychotherapy. The points of contact between the two schools of thought are evident in the language used when discussing these phenomena. For example, psychoanalyst Nathan Field (1989) writes about 'listening with the body', while bodywork psychotherapist Michael Soth (1999) refers to 'the counsellor's body as antennae and barometer'.

In practice, the somatic aspects of the countertransference are almost inevitably entwined with the thoughts and images that drift into the therapist's mind as the client speaks or remains silent. I became particularly aware of this on one occasion when I was working with a young woman whose fine blonde hair was scraped back tightly into a ponytail. So unforgiving was the pressure on her hair that I could see the roots pulling at the skin around her hairline. Sitting in my chair, I experienced simultaneously a feeling of misery and frustration, a fantasy of her hair falling free as the rubber band constricting it was removed, a physical urge to cross the room and remove the band, and a fleeting image of myself doing exactly that.

I am not the first psychotherapist to have discovered that there is usually a rationale for such strong physical reactions and images, a rationale that may not yet be evident in what is being communicated in words. In Roy Schafer's terms, the therapist is responding to a 'showing', which is not yet a 'telling'. Psychological difficulties are finding a physical form, which in turn evokes a powerful response in a sensitive onlooker. This is particularly likely to happen in a psychoanalytically informed setting, where the play of unconscious-to-unconscious communication is at the centre of the proceedings.

We might speculate that, at some level, the client wants the therapist to know what she unconsciously knows herself – the 'unthought known' (Bollas, 1987) of trauma, abuse, neglect, rejection or other pain. The channel of communication in play is the process of projective identification (Klein, 1946), a process elaborated by Bion (1962) in his consideration of pre-verbal communication in infancy. Through projective identification, the client unconsciously informs the therapist about her inner world by stirring up in the therapist feelings similar to her own. Such feelings may be related to present circumstances, or they may have been experienced in the past but denied access to consciousness.

Such phenomena naturally have implications for practice. I have come to recognise in myself certain countertransference responses to clients who, in one way or another, look dishevelled, ill nourished or physically ill at ease. I know that I may find myself feeling sad and hungry, even though lunch time is some way off. At other times, I may feel so low that I can hardly find the energy to speak. Nathan Field states that:

> Some states of fear, rage, longing and hunger may date back to a time when no words were available and psychic trauma could not be distinguished from physical injury. In these cases bodily symptoms in the therapist may provide the first clue to understanding. Thereafter the patient may begin to gain insight into their experience. (1989: 514)

An embodied countertransference response must be counted as being extremely valuable if, as Nathan Field suggests, it can offer a way of knowing something of the quality of a client's very early experience. By reflecting on his or her somatic countertransference responses, the therapist performs the maternal function of joining up the physiological and psychological, described at the very beginning of the book. On this basis, the client is in turn likely to become more able to engage in his or her own 'joining up', linking symptoms and physical activities with memories and states of mind. This activity amounts to the telling and re-telling of a body storyline.

## The case study as research method

> A conscientious, detailed, and interesting report of even a single case is like a fine portrait; we can return to it again and again when we wish to understand. Its helpfulness is in depth rather than in breadth of view. (Cobb, in Sifneos, 1965: xi)

When I was a psychology student, groups of us were involved in experimental research. In our endeavours, we would go to great lengths to 'control' all but one of the variables that might influence a person's performance on a chosen experimental task. We then recruited as large a number of people as possible to take part in the experiment. We hoped to show a statistically significant effect of the one remaining variable, the one that we had decided to manipulate.

For example, two groups of students ('matched' if possible for age, sex, class background, subject being studied and so on) might be asked whether or not they agreed with a certain, perhaps rather socially unacceptable, statement. In the experimental group, according to a pre-arranged plan, four 'stooges' would give the 'unacceptable' answer before the unwitting recruits were asked for their views. In the control group, there would be no stooges. The results could then be compared to see whether the view expressed by a student was significantly affected by the opinions that had previously been voiced. Non-significant results meant that the experiment was a failure. It suggested either that a key variable had not been thought of and controlled, or that the amount of individual difference between the experimental subjects was relatively large and was masking the working of the chosen variable.

A psychoanalytic approach to human behaviour could hardly be more different to the one outlined above. Differences between individuals are not regarded as 'nuisance' elements to be screened out. On the contrary, individual meaning-making, which is what we encounter in our day-to-day work, is the primary source of our understanding. It is through close attention to the individual narrative that we hope to understand how general circumstances translate into individual experience and behaviour.

The 'talking cure' of psychoanalysis has a long tradition as a kind of action research. It is through 'learning from the patient' (Casement, 1982) that psychoanalytic theory has developed and been refined. From the time of Freud's famous case studies, there has been an ongoing 'dance' between clinical experiences – as discussed in supervision, at seminars and conferences, and in written papers – and existing theory.

Michael Rustin has recently re-stated the merits of the clinical case study, referring to this methodology as 'the psychoanalytic equivalent of Pasteur's laboratory' (Rustin, 1997).

Each client's story is individual and particular, yet it can be seen that pattern and meaning emerge over time as certain themes are repeated, both within the narrative of an individual client and between the narratives of a number of different clients.

There is perhaps an inevitable tension between the demand for 'evidence-based' medicine and the ethical position characteristic of psychoanalytic enquiry:

> The control of the outside world routinely sought by normal sciences is made impossible and undesirable for psychoanalysis by its distinctive commitment to the autonomy of its human subjects. (Rustin, in Miller et al., 1989: 62)

But the ethical issues are not the only consideration. Quantitative research has serious limitations wherever there is a need to achieve a more than superficial understanding of motivation and meaning in human behaviour. Even if we could ensure a 'standard environment', then that environment would be experienced differently by each individual according to his or her constitutional make-up and the prior experiences he or she brings to the scene. In the field of health research, the current preoccupation with establishing general rules threatens to blind policy-makers to the specificity and uniqueness of the life of the individual. We should not be surprised, therefore, when initiatives misfire and when programmes of intervention, for example health promotion endeavours, fail to produce the desired results.

## Touching and not touching in psychotherapy

Many readers will be aware of the debate about touching or not touching in psychotherapy, which concerns both the ethical status and the efficacy of 'hands-on' work within the psychotherapy setting. I think it is fair to say that positions have tended to become polarised around rather fixed points of view. A useful review of some of the lines of argument that have been pursued can be found in Kertay and Reviere (1993).

Typically, those who oppose hands-on work in psychotherapy argue that bodywork therapists are missing the point, working unethically or both. On the other hand, bodywork psychotherapists argue that other therapists fail to work with the 'body' or with the 'whole person', a point of view with which I have already taken issue. Having raised the question of how the physiological and psychological become joined up, I feel that I should engage, at least briefly, with the debate about 'hands-on' and 'hands-off' approaches. The question may reasonably be asked: why not encourage the joining up by including physical and verbal work within the one therapy setting?

I would like to draw attention first to a frequent confusion between two different issues: the issue of informal physical contact – shaking hands when a client comes into the room – and the question of formal physical contact, in the form of a massage or a bioenergetics exercise, for example. As far as informal physical contact is concerned, I follow the conventional psychoanalytic practice of keeping such contact to a minimum. However, in common with many colleagues, I do question the validity of a total 'touch taboo'. I would consider it unhelpful and potentially wounding to refuse to respond to a client-initiated handshake.

How helpful is it, though, to offer support or reassurance through informal physical contact, even when such contact falls well within the boundaries of ethical practice? Casement (1982) describes his client 'Mrs B's' request that he should agree to hold her hand to enable her to re-experience a traumatic childhood event. This event involved the young Mrs B being operated on under local anaesthetic, during which procedure her mother fainted. Mrs B remembered feeling terrified as her mother's hands slipped away and she disappeared. Casement is at first inclined to agree to the request but in the end refuses it, despite intense pressure from the client, feeling that in order to work through the trauma, the client needs to re-experience the essential element of the original situation, which involved *not* having her hand held.

In weighing up these matters, we should be wary of assuming that touch can be simply and strictly defined. Symbolic equivalents of touch play a very important role in adult experience. This emerges in our everyday language when we say, 'I was very touched by her sending the flowers' or 'His words touched my heart.' These matters are discussed in more detail in the next chapter. For the moment, I will make the point that 'as if' touching has the potential to enable physiological and psychological facets of experience to become joined up, without the need for a 'hands-on' style of therapeutic intervention.

In relation to the question of formal bodywork interventions, we might ask: how possible is it really to integrate bodywork and verbal approaches within the one therapy setting? Two clients have recently come to my attention, both of whom previously attended sessions with bodywork psychotherapists. The first told her new therapist that she had decided to leave her previous therapist because there was no 'psychotherapy' element, by which she meant that there was no verbal exploration of the physical experiences she underwent. The second complained that the previous therapy was 'just talking', that there was no 'hands-on' work at all, and that she found this confusing because it was not what she had expected.

Such reports suggest that it is difficult to integrate 'being with' with 'doing to'. It is not difficult to see why this might be the case. The bodywork psychotherapist is obliged to move to and fro between the role of listener and collaborator and the role of expert, a difficult transition to manage. Similarly, the client is called upon at one moment to be the initiator, to lead the process through the presentation of his or her material. In the next moment, he or she may be asked to lie down and make certain movements according to the therapist's suggestions or may perhaps receive some kind of massage. Even when we are feeling at our best, such role shifts are difficult to manage.

Beyond the avoidance of these kinds of confusion, most psychoanalysts believe that there are other very real advantages in placing a strict limit on tactile contact. First, the risk of a serious misunderstanding between client and therapist is somewhat reduced. Second, restraint in relation to tactile contact increases the potential for intimacy within the transference–countertransference matrix and the play of unconscious communication. I make this statement on the basis of my belief, borne out by experience, that only a certain level of intimacy can be tolerated and sustained in any particular situation. Beyond this, a person may feel abused, may be obliged to erect defences and to retreat behind them, or both.

It is interesting to reflect that defensive retreats are functional and helpful in some situations. The gynaecologist, who is obliged to touch a patient in a quasi-intimate and sexual manner, usually wears a white coat and adopts a rather formal mode of address by way of compensation. This distancing is experienced as helpful to both parties, at least during the examination. But it is not helpful to provoke such defences in the psychotherapy setting. The therapist who introduces tactile contact into the proceedings must be prepared for a decrease in intimacy in other channels of communication. To do otherwise is to disregard the client's need to safeguard his or her personal boundaries.

The clinical material in the next two chapters offers a window on my own way of working with issues of physicality. My approach reflects the emphasis accorded by Winnicott and later by 'narrative' psychotherapists to the play of ideas and gestures in a dialogue between therapist and client. Interpretation is not regarded (as in classical Freudian and Kleinian psychoanalysis) as the *sine qua non* of the analytic procedure. My attention was drawn to the significance of narratives of physicality ('body storylines') by somatic countertransference experiences and by particular client communications, which both interested and puzzled me.

Such communications involved client descriptions of embarking on a programme of exercise, or taking up a sport, or visiting a complementary therapist for 'hands-on' treatment such as massage, aromatherapy or reflexology. Not surprisingly, as these activities have become a more familiar feature of our contemporary cultural landscape, they have also found their way into client communications in the therapy setting. Large-scale participation in such activities is a relatively recent phenomenon, and as yet few references to them have appeared in the psychoanalytic literature.

What can be found in abundance in the existing literature are accounts of uses of touch and movement activities in situations where they come into the service of pathology. Over time, I have realised that some of my clients use physical activities in a psychologically *helpful* way. Their engagement with exercise is neither obsessional nor overly narcissistic. The activities are being used to establish a more robust sense of embodiment, of evoking body memories of early experiences. Through the process of reflection and dialogue in verbal therapy, we have been able to bring the activities more fully into the service of relationship and self-understanding. The accounts I present here and elsewhere of 'body storylines' and 'beneficial psychosomatic processes' have their origins in these clinical encounters.

# CHAPTER 10

# Touch and Health in Adult Life

Whichever stance we take, we can assume that for each of us our response to touch is rooted in the early experience of touch in our lives and therefore involves all levels of our being. (Eiden, 1998: 1)

*Do adults suffer from touch deprivation, and if so, how does it manifest itself? If a client in counselling or psychotherapy reveals a history of deprivation of responsive and appropriate touch, how can we work ethically and effectively with this material? These questions are discussed below with reference to extracts from psychotherapy work with 'Richard' and 'Linda'. As in Part II of the book, I shall consider client engagement with touch experiences and client use of movement activities in two separate chapters, while acknowledging the affinities between the two modalities.*

I have described a process, with a theoretical underpinning in Winnicott's work, whereby 'good enough' handling ushers in 'good enough' indwelling, which in turn supports both physical and psychological aspects of health. To what extent do the infant needs outlined by Winnicott continue to hold sway in adult life?

Many of us know from personal experience that touching, or being touched by another person, has the potential to enhance well-being. When a skilled masseur works on a client, the client on the one hand relaxes and experiences a general sense of well-being and on the other may experience an increase in somatic awareness, become aware of different areas of the body as they are massaged in turn. The physical sensations evoked may call to mind a number of different thoughts, memories and feelings:

I separated from my husband in my late thirties and the trauma gave me severe neck pain. Painkillers seemed to have no effect so I called my

141

local health club and booked myself in for a massage. It helped my neck enormously and I started to go regularly whenever I felt particularly stressed. I had to get over the initial worry that I was using money I could ill afford to fritter away on myself, but the benefits were enormous to my self-esteem. It was only when I had a regular massage that I realised how very much I missed the tactile side of the relationship I'd had with my husband – someone's arms around you in bed, a hand to hold. (Extract from *Woman and Home*, June 1997)

My concern here is to consider how such a 'joining up' of physiological and psychological experiences can be aided through a process of reflection and elaboration in the psychoanalytic psychotherapy setting.

## Symbolic equivalents of touch

The rationale that touch inhibits the process of symbolising implies that the body is related to the concrete literal level and the mind to the symbolic level only – an outdated dualistic concept. (Eiden, 1998: 2)

On this point, Bernd Eiden, a bodywork therapist, and psychoanalytic psychotherapists are likely to find themselves broadly in agreement. Touch does not happen only at the concrete and literal level. As we grow older, experiences that are *symbolically* equivalent to touch take on an importance of their own.

For example, I might say that I feel 'stung' by a person's harsh words or that a criticism is a real 'slap in the face'; and might I not feel my cheek burning, as if I had indeed been physically struck? There is a fine line between illusion and delusion, and sometimes this 'as if' quality of symbolic touching may be lost. One client clearly showed that his therapist's words felt like physical touch. At times, he would peel and brush the therapist's words off his jacket and flick them away as if he could not bear to have them impinge upon him. For the most part, however, this line is not crossed, and words are experienced as symbolic rather than as actual touch.

Gaze can also count as touch and has the potential to help a person to feel in contact with a source of support and containment. A talk comes to mind, given by the child psychotherapist Dilys Daws in 1999 for the Squiggle Foundation. Referring to her psychotherapeutic work in a baby clinic, Daws described positioning herself for part of the time near the baby weighing scales. Here, she was able to observe how a mother might 'wrap the baby around with her gaze and her voice' while the baby was being weighed, and how this helped the baby to hold himself together through the weighing procedure.

Later in life, gaze also has the capacity to offer a kind of virtual 'handling' that supports the completion of a nerve-wracking task. A child in a school play may falter in the middle of his lines, but turning to the audience and seeing the love and support in his father's gaze, he feels able to continue. If physical proximity were possible, the father might take the child's hand. In that case, we would have no doubt in saying that we were witnessing an incident of touching. The steady supporting gaze that takes the place of physical contact in the example above is an equally identifiable incident of symbolic touching.

Attachment theory offers a useful conceptual framework for considering these matters. The gaze of a parent or other attachment figure signals his or her availability and helps to keep a child's anxiety levels within manageable limits. A 'secure base' (Ainsworth, 1969; Bowlby, 1988) for demanding exploration and endeavour is felt to be in place.

## Touch deprivation in adult life

An underlying sense of lack or insufficiency with regard to touch experiences, of which the sufferer may or may not be consciously aware, can have its origins in present or in past experiences. As we move into middle age, our 'tactile' circumstances change. We are less likely to have young children to attend to, with all the handling that is involved. If we are unlucky enough to lose a long-standing and affectionate partner, we lose the touch experiences that were a part of that relationship, including experiences of sexual touch. We may find it considerably less easy to embark upon a new relationship than we did in our youth.

The overlaps between the receptors and nerve pathways stimulated by touch and movement experiences have already been noted. But as we move into old age, activities involving vigorous movement, which might to some degree substitute for touch experiences, are also likely to tail off. In addition, if we experience a narrowing of our social world, symbolic touch equivalents such as gaze and warm conversation may be less available to compensate for deficits of skin-to-skin touch.

The impact of these changes on health has not been a major area of research, but there is some relevant material. In Chapter 6, I outlined studies suggesting that baby massage carries significant emotional and physiological gains for babies, particularly when they have been born prematurely or have suffered from rough handling or touch deprivation. These same studies have produced evidence that the gains described are not limited to the very young. For example, depressed mothers involved in the programmes said that they themselves benefited from *giving* massage. They found the activity enjoyable, and it made them feel closer to their infants. They also perceived their infants as being easier to soothe. These improvements in the mother's mood and the mother–infant relationship set in motion a kind of 'virtuous circle' (Field, 1995).

In one particular study, grandparents were recruited to take part in a massage programme for neglected and abused infants. These grandparents received massages themselves as part of their preparation for the project, and they were, of course, also trained to give massage. In an unexpected finding, many of the grandparents described themselves as changed by their participation in the project. The symptoms of depression that some had been experiencing significantly diminished, and almost all the participants reported an improvement in mood (Field, 1995). Further research is needed to establish how much of the improvement derived from the sense of making a valuable social contribution and how much derived directly from the touch experiences of giving and receiving massage.

The potential impact of touch deprivation on all aspects of health is beginning to be taken more seriously. In Britain, a project has begun in which volunteers take pets on regular visits to homes for the elderly, to be patted and stroked by the residents. Hairdressing has always been popular in residential homes and hospices, and the non-intrusive experience of 'handling' that it offers is gradually becoming more recognised. In recent years, there has been a growing provision of 'hands-on' therapies, such as massage and aromatherapy, in hospices. Where these services exist, they are well used and much appreciated by the patients (personal communication, I. Bremner, 1999). Post-operative massage is now a fairly widespread practice on general hospital wards, and in Britain the National Health Service has taken the step of engaging a small number of aromatherapists.

We know that there is a relatively high incidence of depression among elderly people, and it seems likely that this is, at least in part, linked to disturbances of indwelling, which have their roots in inadequate touch and touch-equivalent experiences. The role of touch deprivation in elderly and other subsections of the population is a topic that warrants considerably more research than has so far been undertaken.

As far as touch experiences among younger age groups are concerned, health practitioners and social workers are only too familiar with the potentially serious consequences of childhood sexual abuse and of physical abuse and neglect. Many of the clients who come to us in the grip of psychosomatic illness, or with a compulsion towards self-injury or problems involving drugs and alcohol, describe a very poor history of touch. Besides situations that qualify as actual abuse, all kinds of different scenario are encountered in the clinical situation. Maternal handling may have been almost entirely absent, or may have been simply practical and associated with extreme emotional coldness. A woman who regularly injured herself gave this poignant account of her experiences:

> Sometimes no-one spoke to me for weeks. We would pass on the stairs like strangers. There were never any hugs or love, just ice-cold looks, nothing at all. (Arnold, 1995: 16)

Several researchers (summarised in Favazza, 1989a, 1989b) have found that people who injure themselves frequently report feelings of depersonalisation and dissociation. Such research, combined with my own experiences, has led me to suggest that:

> we might see self-harm as a kind of self-attention to the need for handling in order to stay alive. (Turp, 1999b: 317)

This suggestion is compatible with Winnicott's thinking on the meaning of psychosomatic pathologies (among which I include both psychosomatic symptoms and various forms of self-harm, such as eating disorders and self-injury). On many occasions, Winnicott drew attention to the health-seeking nature of such difficulties, expressed in their opposition to a defensive split between the psychological and physical aspects of the self:

> Psycho-somatic illness implies a split in the individual's personality, with a weakness of linkage between psyche and soma, or a split organised in the mind in defence against generalised persecution from the repudiated world. There remains in the individual ill person, however, a tendency *not* altogether to lose the psychosomatic linkage.
>
> Here then is the *positive value of somatic involvement.* (Winnicott, 1966: 113)

To summarise, when a person unconsciously attempts to address damage to or a disturbance of indwelling, this attempt may find expression in a number of different ways. Winnicott refers in the passage cited above to the route of psychosomatic symptoms. Such symptoms oblige the sufferer to attend to the physical self and often to seek help from the outside world. *The body refuses to be forgotten.* In self-injury as well, a part of its meaning may reside in its opposition to the loss of psychosomatic union, which at the experiential level is a loss of feeling real or of feeling sane. Paradoxically, cutting a gash in the skin may bring a sense of being held together when one is at one's most desperate:

> It's a solution that means I'm not going to flip out completely and kill myself. It's something I do for myself, it's mine, a way of feeling I am in control of what I am doing. (Arnold, 1995: 14)

Clients who injure themselves are sometimes able to use the psychotherapy setting to identify less damaging ways of attending to a need for touch experiences. Examples in my practice have included decisions to begin swimming, steam baths, massage and horse-riding. In time, the damaging handling involved in self-harm comes to be replaced by the beneficial handling involved in self-care. The primary therapeutic factor seems to be the gradual internalisation by the client of the therapist, as a figure who holds in mind the client's physical and emotional needs, and who feels concerned that these needs should be met in a non-destructive way.

This process can be assisted by the selection of a body storyline for elaboration within the psychotherapy setting. Where the dialogue between client and therapist is focused in part on the client's use of his or her physicality in the outside world, there is an opportunity for the physiological and psychological aspects of experience to become properly joined up, perhaps for the first time. Through a dialogue centred on physicality, underlying splits between psyche and soma are addressed in the here and now of the consulting room.

## 'Gentle bumps': a case study of Richard

My first example of these processes in action involves a client whom I shall call Richard.

Richard was a man who came to see me at the age of 28, suffering from painful feelings of isolation and describing himself as depressed and beset by feelings of hopelessness. He had a good job in the computer industry. Richard attributed his difficulties to shyness and to a lack of confidence in social situations. He told me that these difficulties meant that he had very few friends and also that he had had very little sexual experience. Although he was quietly spoken, Richard was an articulate person who had no particular difficulty in putting words to his experiences.

A few sessions into our work together, Richard began to speak, with considerable embarrassment, about his behaviour in London underground stations. He told me very hesitantly that on every journey, he engineered a number of 'gentle bumps', small collisions with other passengers. These incidents took place in the corridors and hallways that he traversed when changing trains on his journey to and from work.

I said that I could see it was difficult for him to speak about these matters, but that I thought they were important and that I would like to know more. Richard told me that his strategy was to almost avoid the person coming towards him, then at the last moment to make a very slight adjustment of direction and posture so that the physical contact was made. It was important to him that the collision passed more or less unacknowledged. A 'successful' bump caused no pain to either party, and was not sufficiently significant to warrant an apology. Richard tried to manage six to ten such bumps on each journey. I asked Richard what he made of the situation he was describing, but he clearly had no idea what motivated his behaviour.

My first thought was that these 'bumps' spoke of suppressed feelings of aggression. I thought of Melanie Klein's very young client who 'bumped' figures of horses together in a simulation of sexual intercourse between his parents. I refrained from sharing these thoughts with Richard. It struck me as

I mulled the matter over that something about the quality of the incidents described and of Richard's presence in the room suggested other possibilities. I found myself feeling sad, strangely exposed and uncomfortable. I noticed that I had folded my arms over my chest. I said to Richard:

> 'There is something rather poignant about what you have told me. I don't know at the moment what we should make of it. We shall have to wait and see what sense it makes.'

Over time, a number of thoughts and memories did gradually surface, and a clearer picture began to emerge. I already knew that Richard lived alone and had done so since leaving his family and coming to London to work. Now he told me that whole days went by when he touched no one. The 'bumps' were his only form of human-to-human physical contact. It seemed there was an unconscious plea in Richard's narrative, since I often felt inclined to reach out and gently brush his hand, to make some small physical contact with him. That this would have been contrary to normal psychoanalytic practice was one consideration, but by no means the only one. Thinking about Casement's work with 'Mrs B' (see Chapter 9), I understood that the work properly involved a struggle to remain with Richard's strong sense of yearning and isolation. To attempt to relieve these feelings through physical contact would have deprived Richard of the opportunity to relive the situation as it once was.

I asked Richard if he remembered being held and cuddled as a child. He told me he had been an only child. His parents, he said, were not much given to touching and hugging. His father suffered from asthma and bronchitis, and had been unwell during much of his childhood. These periods of sickness left the family in difficult financial circumstances and his mother often seemed preoccupied with worries, both about his father's health and about making the money go round. We could both see that Richard's touch-deprived situation was not new. On the contrary, it went back a very long time.

Six months into the therapy, Richard began to describe periods of dissociation and depersonalisation. At these times, he experienced himself as 'blank' and 'empty', and was tormented by images of himself as a disembodied 'talking head'. On one occasion, he arrived in an extremely agitated state. Two days earlier, he had happened to see an old *Monty Python* television programme. The introductory sequence included a 'man' who was just a large and bizarre head spouting forth words. Then a foot came down and crushed the head. This image terrified Richard and re-appeared in nightmares on the two following nights. On both occasions, Richard woke up in a panic, remembering only this image and the feeling that he had no body and was about to disappear.

At this point, I felt that Richard was in a very fragile state, and I strongly urged him to increase the frequency of his sessions to twice a week. This suggestion led to the emergence of very negative feelings towards me. Richard questioned the whole point of therapy, saying that I didn't really feel anything for him. I was just earning my living. As we delved into these feelings further, Richard said that he had assumed that I was not really interested in him, but that this was confusing. It seemed to be both true and not true.

I suggested to Richard that the root of the issue might be that, like his mother, I denied him cuddles and kisses and all of the physical affection that a child might rightfully expect from the people close to him. Richard cried when I said this and looked at me longingly. I said that his resentment at this situation was perhaps linked to his denigration of other aspects of our relationship. He had decided that I felt cold towards him and uninterested in him, but at the same time, this point of view did not quite fit with what he was experiencing in the room. These interpretations seemed to bring Richard some relief. His face relaxed and he looked at me in a more friendly, hopeful and trusting way. When he arrived for his next session, he told me that he would like to begin coming twice a week.

Although progress had been made, this was by no means the end of the issue. It gradually became clear that Richard's resentment towards his mother and towards me was echoed in a refusal to give other possibilities for meeting his touch needs any chance of success. On one occasion, Richard began a sexual relationship but managed to sabotage it almost before it had begun by always getting up and going home immediately after intercourse. The encounter lasted only three weeks.

At around this time, I noticed that I had begun to feel uncomfortable and to fidget in my chair when I was with Richard. I couldn't seem to find a position that felt right (even though this would not be a problem with the following client). Richard always sat at one end, the end nearest to me, of the sofa that doubles in my consulting room for a couch. In a characteristic pose, he set himself squarely on the sofa and placed his hands, palms up, on his knees. Feeling that my discomfort in the countertransference must have a meaning, I turned my full attention to the physical elements of the situation.

As he spoke, Richard began to gesture with his hands and he thrust his head forward. His head and hands seemed very large and lively. At the same time, the rest of his body was in retreat from me. Thin and unanimated, pressed against the back of the sofa, it seemed to recede from view. Reflecting silently on my discomfort and on his body position, it occurred to me that Richard was not at all sure how close he wanted me to be. He seemed at the same time to reach towards me and to hang back. The next thought that came to mind was that this was the same mixed message that he had given to his girl-friend when he moved towards her in sexual intimacy but then retreated from her almost simultaneously.

I shared these thoughts with Richard, apparently prematurely, as he made no response at all. However, he returned to the matter in the next session, asking me what I had meant. When I stopped speaking, he nodded thoughtfully. A few minutes later, he began to talk openly about an enormous need for touch and comfort, a 'touch hunger' which he felt could never be met. His need and desire for love and touch were held in a fine balance with a terror of exposing his neediness and vulnerability. Richard went on to make his own links to his terror of the *Monty Python* image. He said he felt so cut off from his body that he feared that he was just a 'talking head'. He felt physically hollow and empty.

At around this time, new memories from early childhood began to come to mind. Richard remembered that any expression of neediness resulted in a look of disdain on his mother's face. Sometimes she told him that 'Little boys must be brave' or seemed deliberately to turn away from his outstretched arms. I asked Richard if he thought I also expected him to be tough and self-sufficient. Looking very tearful, he was able to acknowledge that he did feel cared for by me, and that it was beginning to feel safe to let me see this sad and needy part of him.

In spite of these developments, Richard's 'bumping' activities continued unabated. Matters came to a head when he misjudged his movements and crashed into a female passenger much more forcefully than he had (at least consciously) intended. She became very angry and asked him what the hell he thought he was doing. I told Richard that I thought he wanted me to know how desperate he still felt and reminded him of the things he had told me about his 'touch hunger'. Richard said:

> 'I suppose I do bump into people just not to feel so alone. It's pathetic really, but it's some kind of contact. It makes me feel somehow more real.'

I said to Richard that he had described to me only two kinds of attempt to meet his needs for touch, the 'bumping' on the tube and a rather ill-judged sexual encounter. I wondered aloud why he seemed unable to consider other, less fraught, ways of meeting what had been recognised in therapy as legitimate needs.

The following week, Richard told me, rather grumpily I thought, that he was going to begin to go to t'ai chi classes. A male friend at work was already attending, and he had decided to give it a go. I asked Richard if this decision was related to the comments I had made the previous week, and he confirmed that this was the case. I said, 'Perhaps it felt as if I was telling you, go and sort out your needs for yourself.' Richard smiled ruefully. 'Still', he said, 'I might as well give it a go.'

In fact, Richard enjoyed the classes rather more than he had expected to. He sometimes spoke in therapy about the movements involved, particularly about the exercises undertaken jointly with a partner. At the same time, it was clear that he sabotaged the t'ai chi project in a number of ways. He arrived home in the evening to discover that he had 'forgotten' the class. He arrived late into work on the day of the class so that he was not able to leave in time to make the class. I told Richard that I thought he was expressing his resentment towards me for apparently sending him out into the world. Richard responded by saying that it was, of course, his mother who had sent him out into the world without the resources he needed. I said, 'You both do and don't want to recover. At one level, you would rather continue to suffer.'

After a long pause, Richard said slowly and reluctantly:

> 'But what if I do recover? What if I am OK? Does that mean that my horrible childhood was OK? It was so empty, so thin. Does that have to be enough?'

As he finished speaking, Richard began to cry bitterly and then to sob. For the first time, I felt he was really in touch with his sense of hurt and anger. He was now able to let me see the depth of his pain and to allow himself to feel seen by me.

A major part of the psychoanalytic psychotherapy process consists of holding the client in mind. This holding in mind is expressed in many ways, in the provision of a comfortable and reliable setting, in remembering what has been said and in a certain quality of attention, which involves an openness to nuances of emotion. Infant observation has confirmed that holding in mind is closely linked at the beginning of life with physical handling. Over time, the psychoanalytic setting and the verbal and non-verbal dialogue that took place within it seemed to help Richard to feel held. At the same time, he was able to meet some of his needs for physical handling by doing t'ai chi. Richard's decision to talk about the t'ai chi in the psychotherapy setting seemed to express his need to join up the physical and psychological aspects of the changes he was experiencing.

By the end of the second year, Richard's episodes of bumping and the harrowing interludes of feeling strange, dissociated and disembodied had come to an end. A great deal of the third year of therapy was given over to the process of mourning a childhood that seemed realistically to have been quiet and rather bleak. At the same time, Richard began to feel more hopeful and to voice thoughts about the possibility of moving on.

At the beginning of the fourth year, Richard met a woman, as it happened at his t'ai chi class, and they began a sexual relationship. Things moved forward very quickly from here. After six months, Richard and Marie decided to marry. When Richard left therapy, towards the end of the fourth year, they were expecting their first child. During the last few months of our work together, Richard often began a session by talking about his and Marie's plans. They had both been only children and had felt lonely and isolated as they grew up. In order to protect the expected child from the same experience, they were hoping to have at least two children eventually. They were looking to buy a larger property with these thoughts in mind.

This practical account would soon give way to Richard expressing his excitement and delight at his new situation. He was obviously extremely happy in his marriage and over the moon about the pregnancy. He beamed at me as he told me that he had listened to the baby's heartbeat at the antenatal clinic. He told me with great pride that he made a tape of his favourite tunes and played them to the child in his wife's womb. He said that Marie was healthy and looking great, but that she got very tired during her working day. He had now insisted on taking over most of the housework.

At this point, I became rather concerned about the idealisation of the situation evident in Richard's communications. I suggested that he hoped to undo his own childhood by giving his own child a perfect start, as if this could act as a kind of antidote. Richard said that this was true, that he dreamed of having the baby to rock and to hold, a small being to whom he could give all the things that had been denied to him. After a while, he said to me, 'I know it won't always be like that, though. There will be difficult times as well. Actually, I'm dying to meet this baby, who will be a person in his own right, and to see how it really is.' This session was followed by several sessions dominated by sadness and regret. Richard told me that he thought that nothing could ever make his childhood seem really all right. The best he could do was to ensure that his own child did not feel the coldness that he had experienced. We agreed that this was not 'nothing', that it was some-thing to be valued in its own right.

A month later, Richard described a visit he and Marie had made to see his parents. They were apparently very pleased about the turn that events had taken and were getting quite excited about being grandparents. Richard now recalled in more detail how difficult their circumstances had been during much of his childhood and wondered aloud whether the new baby would also be some kind of a second chance for his parents. Laughing, Richard said, 'Look what you've done to me! I'm starting not to resent my mother. How on earth will I cope?'

This is obviously a very abridged account of the psychotherapy process. So many hours passed by, some of them taken up with Richard's reflections on the steps he was taking outside the therapy sessions to compensate for and transform what had seemed like a very sparse history of touch. These steps included joining the t'ai chi class and then beginning and following through a fulfilling sexual relationship. Through these activities and his work in psychotherapy, Richard retold the story of his touch experiences. He still remembered his mother as cold and undemonstrative, but rather than this being a cause for hopelessness, he now felt that he could change his story in the longer term. He began to see himself as a survivor who had worked hard to recover. And with his recovery came a new sense of compassion towards his parents and the dissolving of his resentment towards his mother.

By the end of the therapy, Richard's body storyline of touch experiences also had a future trajectory, involving fantasised experiences of touching and handling his own baby. These imaginings, which might have been worrying had they appeared in isolation from other changes, were firmly grounded in the steps that Richard had already taken. It was not difficult to believe that, helped by his close identification with his own child, Richard would be to some degree able to enjoy the benefits of feeling handled himself as he handled the infant.

# 'Body-brushing': a case study of Linda

The following piece of work involved an encounter with a 'heavy user' of complementary and esoteric therapies.

Linda, a woman of 30, initially consulted me because she was dissatisfied with her freelance work in the field of costume design. She had originally wanted to be a sculptor and was worried that she had taken a wrong direction. Many of her early therapy sessions were taken up with litanies of complaints about the poor conditions of the contracts she was offered and about the way she was treated by other members of the cast and crew working on a stage or television production. At this time, I felt I could only say that I understood she felt in some way deeply wronged and that the source of that feeling was not yet clear. Linda told me that, when I said this, it was her mother who came to mind. Her mother had worked in theatre herself, and Linda believed that she had regretted the time and energy she had put into raising her three children rather than pursuing her artistic career.

Such was this client's misery and bitterness in relation to her mother that she had not been able to bring herself to visit her parents' home for over a year. She dreaded phone calls from her mother, who, from what I could gather, seemed quite concerned about her. This state of affairs was symptomatic of the many other ways in which she felt stuck and stranded. In spite of her complaints, Linda felt quite unable to contemplate a change of career. Her lease on her flat was about to run out, but she was unable to make housing decisions, which were becoming increasingly urgent. She was in a relationship with a man who, as she put it to me, was 'completely wrong for her', but she continued to let things drift.

Linda was reluctant to discuss any of these themes in depth. She dismissed any comments I made and moved on to the next thing. I understood Linda's dismissive attitude as an attack on our work together, and on me, although she was superficially polite and often enquired after my welfare. Nevertheless, I felt in a difficult situation. Linda's communications made it fairly obvious that she both envied and resented her mother. I had no doubt that these feelings applied to me as well and that her dismissive manner was an unconscious attempt to cut me down to size. At the same time, interpreting this would probably be experienced by Linda as an attempt on my part to cut *her* down to size. My gut feeling was that the therapy had not reached a stage at which these heavily charged dynamics could be articulated and managed.

Soon we had been working together for six months, and I felt that very little progress was being made. While coming for counselling, Linda also embarked upon numerous physical activities – yoga, aerobics, massage, aromatherapy, and then 'body-brushing', a practice that involved brushing her skin all over for five minutes four times a day. Being in the right place at the right time to do the brushing was, of course, an especially complicated business. This was an obsessional activity *par excellence*, a very effective distraction from the pressing problems that Linda faced in her day-to-day life. Pointing this out to Linda was one of a number of interventions on my part that went absolutely nowhere.

As well as the time spent on the activities themselves, Linda used whole sessions to describe to me, often in an esoteric and quasi-mystical language, the wonderful benefits that they brought her. From time to time, she offered me helpful advice, for example to use this or that oil in my bath to alleviate the stress of my work. I said that she must feel she was a terrible strain on me since she felt obliged to spend her own therapy time attending to my welfare. This communication was also brushed aside. Nevertheless, the sound of my own words made me more acutely aware that the sessions with Linda *were* indeed an enormous strain.

A year had passed when, in an attempt to move what felt like a complete log-jam, I interpreted Linda's visits to her other teachers and practitioners in terms of 'splitting'. I hoped that, if this could be taken on board, we might move on to addressing more directly the hostile feelings I suspected Linda of harbouring against me. I suggested to Linda that, by having so many different people to consult, she was avoiding putting all her eggs in one basket, avoiding the possibility of relying upon me and of having to face her mixed feelings towards me. This comment was met with a puzzled and slightly pitying look. Linda went on to speak to me about the healing prop-erties of cider vinegar, and I wondered if her concern was an attempt to atone in phantasy for undisclosed feelings of rage towards me. I realised that I was not confident in the interpretation I had made and did not feel able to pursue it. Linda had not made a favourable or unfavourable comparison between me and the other practitioners. She had not double-booked sessions or missed sessions with me for any reason. The evidence for splitting was, after all, rather flimsy.

Since my external efforts were meeting with so little success, I began to spend more time interrogating my internal world. The word 'agitation' came to mind, and at times I realised that I was working very hard to keep myself from screaming. Why did I feel like screaming when I was in the room with Linda? Were the screams in fact her screams, which she could not express, and if so, what on earth were they about? Thinking about Linda's physical undertakings as a series, rather than individually, it finally dawned on me that Linda might be trying to tell me about some kind of sense of lack and loss in relation to her body. After a while, I shared these thoughts with her, saying that it seemed to me that she kept trying and trying in physical ways to make up for something that was missing, perhaps without knowing what that something might be. I wondered whether her descriptions of her many activities were meant to communicate to me how important this was and what tremendous efforts she was making both to put things right and to let me know about the situation.

There was a long and thoughtful silence. For the first time, I felt that Linda was allowing herself to take something in from me. Eventually, Linda began to speak about being sent away to boarding school at the age of seven. I have no way of knowing whether it was my process of reflection, the words I said, or the intensity with which I said them that made a difference. After a little further hesitation, Linda went on:

> 'I was driven to the school on a cold day and left there. I was taken into the dining room on my own for lunch. I suppose the other girls had already finished eating. I felt terrible and I couldn't really eat. There were cooked tomatoes in the meal. I remember sitting looking at them going cold and congealing on the plate and tears – my tears – dripping down on to them. One of the mistresses said 'Well, if you don't eat it now, you will have to have it again for supper.' I remember a fierce feeling of hatred. Suddenly, I began to cry out loud. I just didn't care any more. I suppose I wanted my mother, and I couldn't understand why I had been brought here and then my mother and father had driven off without me. I don't really remember what happened after that. I must have got over it because after the first year or so I did rather well and I ended up being Head Girl.'

We sat and thought about this together for a long time, and I thought also of my own children when they were seven and eight and nine, images of the cuddles we had and the physical games we played drifting in and out of my mind. I felt very sad and eventually said to Linda that she had not had the physical comfort or the cuddles that a little girl would normally continue to enjoy well beyond the age of seven. I was beginning to understand that her many touch activities might be rather desperate attempts to make up for all that she had missed.

This session marked a turning point in the therapy. For the first time, Linda seemed to feel touched by my words. She cried a great deal in that session and the next, and subsequently seemed subtly different, quieter, more thoughtful, more emotionally in touch. The feeling of stuckness and strain in the room eased and I began to look forward to our sessions together.

Linda began to bring dreams into the session. On one occasion, she dreamt of being at boarding school. She arrived at a class for a lesson only to discover that she had no clothes on. She stood naked and shivering in front of her class mates, feeling unable to move, and nobody came to help her. Talking about the dream, Linda told me that this was exactly how she remembered feeling, as if she had been stripped and left uncovered and that there was no comfort for her anywhere. As Linda allowed herself to remember and re-experience the sense of abandonment she had experienced during her early months at boarding school, she began to see how her feelings of rage had created a desire for revenge against her mother, which was being acted out in their current relationship:

> 'I think I made up this story about my mother being more interested in her career than in me, because it gave me a reason for hating her. (Pause) And perhaps it was less awful than just thinking, well, that she didn't want me at home at all, and there was no other reason for it. I suppose I'm afraid it was my fault.'

'Your fault?', I responded. 'Why?' Linda continued, 'Well, my mother was a very petite woman, and I've always been big and quite strong. I felt she disapproved of that, that she was uncomfortable with how I was.'

I said, 'You think she sent you away because she thought you were too big?' Linda thought for a while. 'No, that's not true at all. The truth is that *I* always hated *her* for being so petite and so poised. It made me feel like a great clumping elephant.' This exchange finally provided the opening for addressing the issues of envy and resentment that had been sitting on the back-burner for so long, and so we entered into another phase in the therapy.

Gradually, Linda came to terms with feelings of envy and resentment, which had been quietly working their evil magic for many years. She saw how much time she had spent sabotaging and spoiling her opportunities, both in therapy and in the outside world. She then embarked on a line of more prac-tical questioning about why she and her two brothers had all been sent away from home at such a young age. Half way through her second year of therapy, she made a visit to her parents' house. As planned, Linda managed to talk to her mother about being sent to the boarding school. Linda's mother told her, in a way that obviously caused Linda to believe her, that she had hated to let her go and had missed her dreadfully. She had felt unable to go against Linda's father's advice, which was that Linda should not miss out on the best educational opportunity available. This conversation brought a great deal of relief to both participants. Mother and daughter cried a great deal, Linda's mother also expressing a great deal of sadness at Linda's rejection of her over the years.

As time went on, Linda managed her difficulties in her career rather better, although she still contemplated an eventual change of direction. In due course, she sorted out her housing situation, as most people do. She finished the unsuitable relationship and soon afterwards started a new one, which was much more enjoyable. As it turned out, these issues were not particularly important. The main work had been done, and I was happy with her decision to leave therapy at the end of two years.

In a phrase that became well known in psychoanalytic circles, Bion cautioned the therapist to embark upon each new session 'without memory or desire'. For a long time, I had failed to heed this advice in my work with Linda. On the lookout for more commonly encountered psychoanalytic themes, I failed to pick up on the sheer physical deprivation that Linda had suffered as a young child. Fortunately, by repeatedly talking about activities involving movement and touch, Linda brought this oversight to my attention, and we were able to put things back on track.

If I had given them more weight, my sense of frustration and the feeling that I wanted to scream might have alerted me rather sooner to the over-developed 'false self' which I was encountering in the consulting room. This competent and socialised aspect of Linda had taken her from being an enraged and crying abandoned child to being Head Girl. In the consulting room as well, misery and fury were suppressed, hidden behind a polite, appreciative and concerned demeanour. Although I had intimations of this state of affairs, Linda's intelligence and apparent concern for me made it particularly difficult to name and engage with the primitive feelings that lay beneath the surface.

It is possible to look at Linda's engagement with body-brushing, aromatherapy, yoga and massage in a number of different ways. First, they seemed directly related to issues of touch deprivation and consequent difficulties in retaining a good sense of psychosomatic indwelling. Body-brushing in particular was both soothing and stimulating. It involved episodes of self-handling at very regular intervals, rather like a feed or a change of nappy. Behind this self-handling, we can identify an unconscious endeavour to contact 'the alive-ness of the body tissues and the working of body functions' which Winnicott (1960a) identifies as the 'true self' element and as the source of the sponta-neous gesture. Second, taken in combination with the advice I was offered, the activities expressed an impulse to undermine the psychotherapy process itself, to compete with and denigrate the work we were undertaking. Third, the description of the activities was a communication to the environment, in this case to me, that there were pressing matters that could only be alluded to indirectly, through a description of 'showings' rather than through a direct 'telling'. Linda needed me to recognise her deprivation and to enable her to feel metaphorically touched by my understanding. Once this has happened, references to body-brushing became more spasmodic and eventually disap-peared from the therapeutic conversation.

I am sure that this list does not exhaust the possibilities. When a narrative has become inscribed in a bodily way, the physical activi-ties that are described are capable of carrying an enormous variety of different meanings, all of which remain to be discovered in the individual work between client and psychotherapist.

I hope that these two case studies offer a more tangible picture of the elements of psychoanalytic practice that I described at the beginning of the chapter. These include working with somatic aspects of the countertransference, enabling a client to feel 'touched' without making physical contact and reflecting with the client on images and emotions arising from touch-related activities being undertaken outside the therapy setting.

# CHAPTER 11

# Physical Exercise and Emotional Well-being

The True Self comes from the aliveness of the body tissues and the working of the body functions, including the heart's action and breathing. (Winnicott, 1960a: 149)

*Exercise may come into the service of both healthy and pathological tendencies. Where it is being used beneficially, it can be thought of as a form of self-care or 'self-handling' which sustains a good quality of psychosomatic indwelling. This chapter presents a general overview of the meanings that exercise may carry in different historical and cultural contexts. It explores the potential psychological benefits of exercise with reference to psychotherapy work with 'Betty' and 'Sheila'.*

Few people would dispute the assertion that physical exercise brings physical benefits, including protection against heart disease and circulatory problems, and an improvement in the functioning of the body musculature and internal organs. We are also familiar with the *negative* psychological possibilities of exercise, in situations in which it comes into the service of an excessively controlling or a self-punitive behaviour. But the *potential psychological benefits* of physical exercise have not as yet been subject to the same thoughtful and detailed discussion.

## 'Use' and 'abuse' of exercise

Physical exercise comes into the category of what I call 'essentially physical' activities (see also Chapter 12). In general, I do not consider it helpful to make a sharp division between 'physical' and 'mental' activities, a division that would echo the dualistic notion of separate entities of 'body' and 'mind'. All activities can be seen to have their physical aspects. As I type these words, synapses are being jumped and chemical transmitters are being released, while externally my fingers are moving up and down on the keyboard. But whether I type the words, write them by hand or dictate them to someone else makes no essential difference to the text produced. The physical aspects of the activity of writing are not important.

However, if we take an activity like swimming or running, the situation is rather different. I call these activities 'essentially physical' because they are brought into being and defined by their physical aspects. The same applies to an activity such as massage, which qualifies as an 'essentially physical' touch experience. What makes something an 'exercise activity' is the primary involvement of movement, often vigorous and rhythmic movement.

At the same time, physical exercise cannot be precisely demarcated. It combines at various margins with sport (compare swimming for pleasure or exercise with swimming in a competitive event), with the enjoyment of our environment (consider a long country walk), with a more spiritual quest (for example, in yoga) and with aesthetic expression, as in dance. In addition, although current developments in technology and working practices push us towards an ever more sedentary lifestyle, some people still undertake energetic physical work, either as their paid work or as part of a leisure activity such as gardening. What I have to say applies to the physical exercise elements of all these activities, as well as to the more obvious examples of running or working out in a gym.

I think it can be fairly convincingly shown that physical exercise can come into the service of both beneficial and pathological tendencies. My own practice reflects both of these possibilities. Below, I present the story of 'Betty', a client who used the activity of running in an increasingly creative manner, to assist in the recovery of a sense of indwelling and of 'feeling real'. I have also worked with clients with a history of exercise abuse. 'Sheila', for example, presented later in this chapter, described how she had run compulsively on the spot in the toilets of the in-patient unit where she had been hospitalised in order to 'work off' the food she had been forced to eat. It is interesting that during the course of our work together, she was able to begin another exercise activity – swimming – which was not abused.

Psychoanalytic accounts have tended to focus on the pathological, on exercise abuse. This is presumably because, in the past,
abuse is what has most frequently come to light when the matter of
exercise has been raised by a client in the psychotherapy setting. A
contribution from J. de la Torre gives the flavour of the traditional
psychoanalytic viewpoint:

> For many young adults – and some who are not so young – attendance
> at a health club, assiduous participation in aerobics, and a daily walk in
> the park demand quasi-religious belief and dedication as well as a fear
> of transgression. (1995: 236)

Exercise, like all behaviour, is embedded within a social and
cultural context, and it is important to recognise that there have
been major shifts in recent years. As the physical demands of
everyday living have diminished, it has become much more
common for people to seek out some form of physical exercise.
This change, as we would expect, has been reflected in the material emerging in the consulting room. We hear more frequently
from clients that they have joined a gym, or taken up aerobics, or
started jogging, or engaged a personal trainer.

It is impossible to generalise about the meanings that are
inscribed into these activities, which differ from one individual to
another and which change over time. Nevertheless, my impression
is that currently, at least in London, exercise is more often than not
used in a psychologically beneficial manner. For the most part, it
seems motivated not so much by a fear of transgression as by a
need to bring into balance our mental and physical exertions, an
endeavour which I see as being linked to an unconscious attempt
to sustain or recover a good quality of psychosomatic indwelling.
Different kinds of motivation may, of course, coexist. Where the
question of use or abuse hangs in the balance, then the way in
which the narrative of exercise activity is worked with in
psychotherapy is likely to have a crucial influence on the outcome.

The beneficial psychological possibilities of physical exercise are
not yet fully reflected in the psychoanalytic literature. For this
reason, all the case studies in this chapter relate to uses of
exercise that are either beneficial from the start or that lend themselves to becoming beneficial through their exploration in the
psychotherapy setting. Narcissistic considerations and fears of trans-

gression are, of course, always relevant. We inhabit a world in which appearance is, perhaps to an unprecedented degree, bound up with status and success. In addition, the government and the media regularly urge us to exercise more, warning of the well-documented health risks of a sedentary lifestyle, and such messages can fuel a self-punitive tendency in some individuals. At best, we remain alert to the possibility that exercise may be being abused without losing sight of the psychologically beneficial possibilities.

# Research findings from exercise psychology

Because its enquiries are not limited to people who are in trouble and seeking help, psychology research circumvents the pathological bias that can skew perceptions within the field of psychotherapy. On the whole, the relevant research supports the view that, among the general population, exercise is most often used in a psychologically beneficial way; exercise abuse is relatively uncommon.

In the course of researching a journal paper (Turp, 1997), I discovered that there are literally hundreds of relevant studies in the psychology literature, of which I will cite just a few. Berger and Owen (1992) found that college students participating in swimming and yoga classes recorded lower scores on anger, confusion, tension and depression measures than did control (lecture class only) students. O'Brien and Conger (1991) conducted a research study involving men and women aged 55–86 years old. They found that participation in sport and physical recreation was significantly associated with 'a general optimism in life orientation'. Berger et al. (1988), in an experiment that randomly assigned participants to a 'jogging', 'relaxation response', 'group interaction' or 'control' group, found that jogging performed best in helping subjects to reduce short-term stress. Many similar studies show benefits with regard to health, mood state, stress level and self-esteem consequent upon taking up some kind of physical exercise.

The motivation of exercisers has also been extensively investigated. One large study (Berger et al., 1988) found that 'enjoyment' and 'having fun' were the reasons most commonly given for engaging in leisure exercise. Improved performance, the safeguarding of health and a desire to enhance physical appearance have also emerged as important motivators. These and similar findings (see, for example, Weinberg et al., 1993) suggest that narcissism and a fear of illness are just two out of a whole range of motivating factors involved in leisure exercise. In contrast to what we might expect on the basis of de la Torre's account, the most frequently cited reasons for exercising are *'enjoyment'*, *'having fun'* and *'feeling better'*.

## Exercise and self-expression

Exercise activities, along with psychosomatic symptoms, have tended to be regarded within psychoanalysis as 'flights from thinking' (McDougall, 1989). This does not do them full justice, since physical 'showings' can quite easily coexist with thinking and with verbal 'tellings'. In health, these two versions of self-expression are complementary rather than mutually exclusive, and various aspects of self-expression go hand in hand. For example, tears are undeniably 'of the body' but can also eloquently express emotion, the feelings involved also lending themselves to expression in words. We may literally 'jump for joy' when we receive exceptionally good news. This does not prevent us speaking about the situation, perhaps saying, 'Fantastic! I got the job!', even as we jump. I concur with Winnicott's view that it is only in cases of damage to the inherent integrity of the psyche-soma that we are likely to see activities or symptoms standing in opposition to symbolisation in words.

Where strong emotions are aroused, words alone, even taking account of the potential variations in their physical elements of tone, volume and intensity, may fall short of what is needed in terms of the immediate management of the situation. In the film of Jane Austen's *Sense and Sensibility*, Colonel Brandon pleads with Elinor, sister of his beloved Marianne, who seems to be at death's door:

> Give me a task, or I shall run wild!

He is duly despatched on an errand and rides off on his horse.

We shall have no difficulty in identifying other film or book scenes in which the protagonist, having faced some major frustration or disappointment, sets off into the forest at a great rate, or sweats his way through a fiercely competitive game of squash. In these examples, there seems to be an acknowledgement that exercise can provide a safe context for 'kicking out', enabling us to steer clear of more destructive or self-destructive actions. We might regard this as a useful form of 'self-handling', calling up the maternal activity of facilitating our physical self-expression while at the same time keeping us from harm. Contemporary psychoanalyst Barry Richards makes this point with reference to the relationship between maternal care and the activity of playing football:

> This modification of aggressive energies (in the game of football) is perhaps aided by our memories of how as babies we express vigour and obtain pleasure through kicking movements, as well as using our feet to struggle against a restraining parent. (1994: 34)

## Experiences of muscle and skin

An exerciser's enhanced sense of skin and muscularity may be psychologically helpful at a variety of different levels. In a general way, vigorous exercise can serve as a bodily reminder of a growing sense of agency and resourcefulness. At a time of crisis, it has the potential to mitigate against a sense of helplessness and to prevent a person from feeling completely overwhelmed.

I referred briefly in Chapter 7 to T. Berry Brazelton's observation that:

> when confronted with a mere object, the baby is jerky and uncoordinated, approaching the object with haphazard snatching movements. (Brazelton, 1975: 29)

Human contact brings about a change in the baby's movements. When the mother makes contact with him, the movements become 'smooth, rhythmic and circular'. I want to make the additional point that 'smooth, rhythmic and circular' movements are characteristic of almost all physical exercise activities. This applies, for example, to walking, running, riding a bicycle (on the road or in the gym), dancing, swimming or digging the garden. In a reversal of the process described by Brazelton, the repetition of such movements perhaps evokes 'memories in feeling' (Klein, 1957) of the loving and attentive contact with which they were first associated. Where this is the case, the exercise activity can be recognised as 'object related', linked to early experiences of handling, rather than primarily narcissistic.

Before moving on to the case studies, I will return briefly to the question of inadequate physical handling in infancy. For the person who has responded to inadequate care with a collapsed physique, expressing an underdeveloped sense of skin, or as Stephen Briggs describes it a 'porous skin', physical exercise provides an opportunity to build a sense of alive self-holding, through an improvement in posture and general vigour. Adopting the physical postures that would normally have come into being and been supported by good maternal handling may give us a belated but nevertheless helpful experience of 'good enough' handling. These possibilities form part of the potential psychological value of 'self-handling' through participation in exercise.

For a person who has experienced abuse and who has become rather tough and self-sufficient, exercise may simply be another manifestation of a toughened and impermeable 'second skin' (Bick, 1968). But there are more hopeful possibilities as well, which can only be evaluated on a case-by-case basis. Sometimes (as in the case of Sheila, described later on in this chapter) exercise emerges in the context of a new concern with self-care, of a kinder relationship to one's own physicality.

Our culture, with its relatively restricted opportunities for close physical contact and with its increasing emphasis on mental activity and mental work, provides few opportunities for reparative work where handling has been inadequate or abusive. For city-dwellers in particular, joining a gym and perhaps engaging a personal trainer – somebody to guide and encourage while protecting against over-exertion – may be an important part of the psychological recovery process.

## Some meanings of running: a case study of Betty

I would like to present a piece of clinical work concerning issues of 'false self' (Winnicott, 1960a) and 'false body' (Orbach, 1995), one which illustrates how the body storyline can provide a thread through client material.

A woman aged 42, whom I shall call Betty, came to see me as a private client. During our first meeting, she struggled for words to describe what was troubling her, repeating several times, 'I just don't know.' She said, 'I could be anybody. I have no idea what I am like.' I asked whether these were new thoughts and sensations. Betty said that, on the contrary, *they went back as far as she could remember*.

As well as having a full-time job in a bank, Betty was a single parent of two boys, aged 14 and 12. Although the boys saw their father for holidays, Betty looked after them most of the time. She described a very busy life, saying, 'I do things the whole time. I'm always busy getting things done. I'm like a machine, really.' I echoed the words 'You're like a machine' and noticed as I said it that Betty *looked* rather machine-like. She sat very square and upright in the chair. Although she was quite animated, her movements were jerky, short and clipped rather than long and expansive. At the same time, I noticed that I was sitting square and upright myself and taking less time than usual to simply be with the client. My breathing was shallow and I felt under an internal pressure to respond quickly.

I asked Betty if she could say more about being like a machine, which led to her saying that she drove herself like a car and just got on with things 'on automatic', in response to the many practical demands made upon her. I asked her if that meant that she took very little time to think about herself, to consider how she felt. She agreed that this was the case, and I said that some things could only be known by consulting within oneself. This comment reflected my own realisation of a need to *look within myself* rather than to 'get on with the job' in the consulting room.

As Betty described her constantly busy life, I felt moved to point out that she had created a *bubble of space for herself* in choosing to come for psychotherapy. This seemed to me significant and something of an exception to her usual way of being. Now we both fell into more of a reverie. Betty said slowly, 'A bubble of space... Yes, that *isn't* like me' and looked slightly tearful. Then she quickly pulled herself together and apologised, saying that she had been a bit down this last few weeks. In these moments, I caught a glimpse of real despair, buried beneath a competent and reliable persona and a warm social manner. Betty and I went on to work together for three years, meeting for sessions once per week.

Quite early on, Betty (who looks neither over- nor underweight) tells me she has been on a number of diets in order to lose weight. As we discuss this issue, her account turns out to be something of an understatement. In fact,

Betty is always on a diet. We establish that she *never* chooses a meal on the basis of what she feels like eating. Instead, she vets its calorific and fat content, tots up her scores for the day and then decides what she is allowed to eat. Betty describes these activities to me as another thing that is 'on automatic' and as 'a kind of constant background noise'. She tells me in a despondent tone that they have been going on 'for years and years'.

I am struck by Betty's despondent tone of voice and feel unusually protective towards her. I make the suggestion that she may feel, in some way, very neglected because she makes so many decisions without any regard to her own enjoyment. Betty thinks about this for a while, then makes a connection to our earlier discussion about machines. As she says to me, in a joking tone, 'One does not consult a machine about its needs. All machines are more or less the same.' Again, there is a long silence; then I ask Betty if she can imagine what it would be like to live more fully within her body, to consult her appetite and her preferences and to act accordingly. Betty slumps a little, looks worn down and stares at the floor. I hear her say, almost inaudibly: 'Why would I do that?'

By this time, Betty has given me an outline description of her family. Her father is described as an evasive man. 'He often worked late or buried himself in a book. He didn't seem very interested in us girls.' Her mother was 'very strict and domineering'. In the next session, Betty goes on to say with considerable feeling, 'I was so afraid of my mother. Later I hated her, but I never let her know. In all these years, I've never asked her to look after the boys. She doesn't understand how to love a child.' My comment 'She didn't know how to love you?' brings a snort of derision. 'That was the last thing on her mind. She just wanted to make sure that we didn't step out of line. As long as we did what she said and made a good impression, that was all that mattered.' Betty sits looking at the floor and struggles not to cry. Eventually, I say sympathetically that, in such circumstances, there is not a lot of point in consulting within oneself. To follow one's own feelings would be likely only to lead to trouble. Betty begins to cry more openly and there is a sense of great relief in her tears.

It seems to me that Betty probably started to cut off from her somatic self, her 'true self', which Winnicott cites as the source of spontaneous feelings, during her childhood years. Her body is often experienced as being cut off and dead, as a 'not me' item which does not confer on her a sense of authentic being. A passage written by Susie Orbach illuminates the processes that might be in play here:

As Winnicott writes: 'The False Self is built on identifications'. So, too, I suggest, is the female false body built on identifications. It is an identification that builds up a bodily sense that is both real and unreal. It is what the girl, later the woman, has to rely on as her body and yet it lacks authenticity, wholeness or reliability. It is both of her and not of her. (Orbach, 1995: 6)

Betty carries within her a very critical and prohibitive voice, which derives primarily from her experiences as a girl. It very difficult for her to be spontaneous, which would involve being in touch with something that feels real and comes from inside. Betty's obsessive pattern in relation to food seems to be one aspect of this scenario. Quite frequently, she returns to the subject of her diets, saying that she wants to make a change, thinking that it might help her to find her 'real self'. But whenever she comes to the point of actually giving up her counting and vetting, she becomes quite terrified. When I ask her what she thinks might happen, Betty becomes breathless and hugely anxious. 'I don't know. *Anything* might happen. Anything at all.'

We reflect together that counting and restricting have become old friends, as well as old enemies. Betty admits that she would 'feel altogether unsafe' without them. I notice that I am feeling anxious and that my own breathing has become somewhat constricted. I ask Betty to tell me a little more about the sense of danger she is hinting at. Betty says, 'I had to be careful. My first concern was not to upset my mother. Often she lost her temper for the smallest thing, like me not remembering where I had put my gloves. I don't think I ever *just did something*. First I would try to judge what mood she was in and whether it would make her angry, which meant I would get slapped and shouted at and then she would sulk for days – not look at me or speak to me. The atmosphere in the house – I can't describe it. Tension you could cut with a knife. Everyone leaning on me to 'apologise to mother' so that 'things could get back to normal... You could hardly breathe.' This revealing communication opens up an opportunity to consider how Betty might be trying to please me and how fearful she might be of my imagined disapproval. We also log the fact that Betty almost ceases to breathe when she is at all anxious and that this makes her feel more dissociated from herself and even less 'real'.

Over these first six months of therapy, I am pleased to see that Betty has become somewhat more animated. She tells me with great feeling that she feels more and more frustrated with being hemmed and hedged in by her self-imposed restrictions. One day, she announces that she has decided to start a daily run. I ask her how that decision has come about, and she tells me: 'Running will keep me in trim. If I can believe that, if I can let that be enough, then maybe I can ease up on the diets.' I say, 'It sounds as though you hope running will wean you off the diets. I shall be interested to know how you get on.'

The next week, Betty tells me that she has started a daily jog, described as 'a boring grind to and from the local park'. I wonder to myself whether this is the beginning of another obsessional activity. It seems most likely at this point that running will fall into a 'compensatory' category of psychosomatic processes, one self-enforced and mechanical activity being exchanged for another. At the same time, the thought crosses my mind that the psychotherapy process may have enabled Betty to use exercise differently from the way in which she uses food. Perhaps she may, after all, be on the point of moving away from a style of self-restriction that has been going on for years. This thought comes from the interest and curiosity that I feel rather than from my rational evaluation of the situation. An image comes to mind of Betty puffing and panting, and I remember her words that she was 'hardly able to breathe' at home. However, somewhat to my chagrin, Betty makes no further mention of running for several months.

Over this period, I notice that Betty is beginning to look different. I have a sense of more flowing movements and of more vitality, of a sense of energy without strain. One day, she tells me about a particularly enjoyable weekend with her two sons, that ended up with them eating at Burger King on Sunday. I say that things must have changed a bit on the diet front if she is now able to go to Burger King. Betty says, 'Well, now I'm running so much, I have a different attitude to food. I have to make sure that I eat enough good things.' I express pleasure and surprise at this hard-won change and go on to say that, as far as I can remember, she has now been going running for four or five months. I add that I remember it was quite tedious at the start.

Betty laughs and says, 'I'd forgotten saying that. Oh no, it's not a bore at all now. I just love it.' We think about this, and Betty realises that, almost imperceptibly, the feeling and meaning of running has completely changed for her. 'I started it to control my weight but now I do it *just for me*. I have so much more energy, actually. My problems haven't gone away but somehow they don't get me down in the same way. I go every morning that I can and I just feel so different.' I am struck by the phrase '*just for me*' and say what a big change that seems for Betty. There is a long silence and then Betty begins to speak with enormous regret of all the years she has spent living for others, never able to just be herself, always 'putting on a show'. This ushers in a series of painful sessions in which Betty allows herself to know how humiliated and belittled she felt when she was growing up, and how fundamentally those experiences have affected her enjoyment of life as an adult.

A few months later, Betty returns again to the subject of running. She says she has started running with a group of other women, and she clearly wants to tell me what good fun this is. We spend some time thinking about this new development. Now running is not only '*just for me*' but also stands as a metaphor for taking up a larger space in the outside world. Betty and her friends enjoy a sense of being a substantial presence in the park. I notice again that Betty looks very different from when I first met her, taller, more confident, more relaxed.

Towards the end of our third and final year together, Betty tells me she is thinking of starting to train for the London Marathon. She has made contact with a charity which is interested in sponsoring two women from her group. 'My parents won't even speak about it. They are totally disapproving. My sons tease me but they let me know they are really proud.' The recognition that her sons love her and do not find her wanting brings tears of pleasure to Betty's eyes.

By this time, I would say that Betty has attained a good quality of psychosomatic indwelling. This achievement is evident in a full emotional range, in an attitude towards food and exercise that emphasises enjoyment, and in Betty's appearance, which now speaks of confidence and of openness to experience. Running, which could so easily have been another obsessive and mechanical activity for Betty, has in the event been transformational, not least as a result of our consideration of its meanings and associations in the therapeutic setting.

I have drawn attention in this case study to my unconscious physical mirroring of the client. I realised, for example, that I had almost stopped breathing when Betty was very tense and then she said the words, 'You could hardly breathe.' Such unconscious mirroring is part of our receptivity to the communications of others. Where we are alert to it and prepared to reflect on its meaning, it serves as an antidote to the danger of the analytic encounter becoming a formulaic process (see Ogden, 1997).

In the same way that we may sometimes find ourselves unconsciously mirroring the client, there is little doubt that the client in turn mirrors the therapist. This is sometimes noticeable when we see a client adopt one of our own gestures. Over time, the gesture may be dropped or the client may transform it into something different, which is her own. This process can sometimes be observed over a period of a few weeks. In my experience, such a development almost always coincides with a strengthening of the therapeutic alliance.

## Swimming: a case study of Sheila

The activities of 'gentle bumping' and 'body-brushing' in Chapter 10 involved movement – walking into the other person and wielding the brush – as well as touch, but it seemed clear that the touch experience was the primary objective; the movement aspect of the activity was more or less incidental.

In the case of swimming, the situation is much more evenly balanced. The experience of moving in a large pool of water is in many ways a touch experience, involving a feeling of being carried or supported, sensations of cold or warmth, the flow of moving water over bare skin, and afterwards the towelling dry. In other ways, it is decidedly a movement experience, involving the coordinated and sometimes vigorous use of all parts of the body. The resulting stretching of the skin and muscles and the involvement of proprioception are part of the 'inner touch' experience, which is a potential of all movement activities.

Winnicott seemed to recognise the special quality of swimming. In the following passage, he associates the activity of swimming with maternal care:

> When we provide a swimming pool and all that goes with it, this provision links with the care with which the mother bathes her infant, and with which she generally caters for the infant's need for bodily movement and expression, and for muscle and skin experiences that give satisfaction. (Winnicott, 1962: 69)

Although he does not use the Kleinian terminology, Winnicott intimates that the activity of swimming has the capacity to arouse memories in feeling of being bathed and attended to in infancy. The rhythmic kicking involved in swimming may also serve to remind the swimmer of the feeling of kicking as a baby and perhaps of the responses evoked by his or her movements. Given the presence of this range of potential conscious and unconscious associations, it would not be surprising to discover that swimming can play a very special part in the preservation or recovery of a good quality of psychosomatic indwelling.

Sheila's childhood circumstances were more obviously disturbing that those described by Richard, Linda or Betty. Born in the North of England, Sheila was an only child whose mother died when she was twelve. Unable to recover from the loss of his wife, her father took to drinking heavily. He was able to hold down his job but was never home in the evenings. Sheila was left to more or less bring herself up. An uncle befriended Sheila, calling round to see her and helping her with her homework. This uncle soon began to sexually abuse her, the abuse continuing until Sheila was sixteen, at which point she left school and home and travelled to London.

Helped by a slight figure, delicate features and her natural acumen, Sheila succeeded in getting a job as a receptionist in a very smart London hotel. In the place of her real past, she invented a past for the benefit of her colleagues, and perhaps also for herself, saying that her parents had recently moved to Australia to live near her (invented) older brother and their two grandchildren. Sheila made no further contact with her father and did not give him the address of her rented one-room apartment.

These are the bare bones of Sheila's history. When she arrived in my consulting room, she was 23 years old and painfully thin. She told me almost immediately that she had a history of anorexia going back over five years. Her eating disorder had twice become so severe that she had twice been admitted to hospital. When she first consulted me, she had just emerged from her second, six week, hospital stay, which had been precipitated by her dangerously low body weight. Neither of us knew how long her recovery might take. In the end, we worked together for 7 years. The work described below took place mainly during the second year of psychotherapy.

At this time, Sheila's relationship to food was very bizarre, although she had managed to avoid any further hospital admissions. She had spent much of the first year of therapy describing to me what she did, and did not, eat. I can summarise by saying that, essentially, Sheila ate very little, never consuming what we would normally think of as a 'meal'. She would only eat 'pappy' food, white bread, flavoured yoghurt, mashed potato and ice cream. She would only eat on her own in the flat, and this seriously curtailed her social life. She was embarrassed by an excessive amount of body hair, which was a side effect of her anorexia. She had not had a menstrual period for over two years.

I felt very moved by Sheila's story of her childhood and by her struggle to make a success of her life. Over the first year of our work together, I discovered that Sheila had a 'gritty' quality and a very good sense of humour. Although she was very ill, and although the prognosis for eating orders of this severity is rather poor, I was able to feel hopeful for her. My concern for Sheila and my respect for her struggles helped to build an alliance between us, which in turn enabled Sheila to voice feelings of murderous envy towards almost everybody. She would rage to me about the lousy hand she had been dealt in life. Other children had a mother to love them. Other children had a father who was some use to them and who protected them from harm. Why had she drawn such a short straw? Everybody, it seemed to her, got more love and care than she did.

An eating disorder can form a part of many different narratives. In Sheila's case, the desire to take complete control, to 'begin again' as if the past had not happened, was a striking feature of her way of managing her difficulties. Self-denial was also an important theme. Sheila denied herself not only the enjoyment of food, but also the enjoyment of sociability. Outside working hours, Sheila lived a very isolated life. She told me that she saw no real prospect of a good sexual relationship or a family life. Envy and self-denial were entangled in a complex way, each fuelling the other. At one point, I suggested to Sheila that her eating disorder was designed to communicate the following message to me and to the world in general:

> 'You haven't looked after me enough and I'm damned if I'm going to do it for myself. I won't give you the pleasure of seeing me thrive, but will force you to see instead that I am hungry and neglected.'

It was half way through the second year of our work together that the matter of sex began to be discussed in earnest. Sheila had moved on sufficiently to be aware of a feeling of yearning for love and physical affection. She began to create opportunities to meet a potential partner, going out with her colleagues for an occasional drink and joining an evening class to learn Italian. By this time, she was also able to go out for a meal, as long as the restaurant was vegetarian and had one of her few 'permitted' dishes on offer.

Over the course of a few months, it became clear to us both that the moment a man showed any interest in her, Sheila retreated from her desires and made herself unavailable. These manoeuvres were rationalised in terms of the man being too young, too old, too dim and so on. Then Sheila decided that perhaps, after all, she might be more inclined towards a woman partner. But she made no effort to meet other gay women, and she only ever spoke of sexual feelings towards men. After going around these circles many times, Sheila admitted that she felt completely stuck. Her desire for a 'soul mate' was being countermanded by intense feelings of fear and distaste, which rose up whenever the possibility of a sexual relationship came into view.

Shortly after this phase, Sheila began to mention that she wanted to start to go swimming. This wish was far from easy to translate into action. Changing into her costume and feeling exposed to the eyes of others were some of the difficulties that were discussed in therapy. Some astute detective work on Sheila's part uncovered a health club that had individual changing cubicles, private showers and a very short walk between the changing facilities and the steps into the pool. At last, she was able to 'take the plunge'. Swimming soon became a regular feature of Sheila's week and of our conversations in therapy. Sheila would tell me that she had been swimming, or that she had not managed to fit in a swim, or then a week later that she had gone back to swimming. I let her know that I recognised that swimming had a special importance for her. Although I did not say so, I was concerned that she might be using swimming in an obsessional way or self-punitive way. Would she eventually reveal that she was meticulously counting lengths and calculating calories?

To my relief, my anxieties proved to be unfounded. What Sheila in fact described was the sensation of water on her bare skin. 'Not quite as good as being touched', she said, 'but almost'. As our dialogue continued, it became clear that Sheila was using swimming to support her contact with her own sensuality, at a time when she felt unable to move towards a sexual relationship. Because of the predominance of physical and primitive elements in sexual relations, the maintenance of this aspect of her sense of self depended on physical rather than on verbal self-expression.

Sheila told me it felt good to be using her body, and that she was feeling stronger and fitter. And, indeed, she began to look healthier, more energetic and not quite as thin. In the sessions, I linked the swimming to other aspects of Sheila's growing willingness and capacity to take care of and to enjoy herself. Sheila's enjoyment of food continued to improve. She managed to initiate and keep up a programme of good dental hygiene, and to visit the dentist. This was no small matter, as her teeth and gums had suffered terribly from her disturbed diet.

Sheila would at times again feel overcome by feelings of envy and hatred. A male colleague at work got promoted and she did not. Sheila complained vehemently about the unfairness of the world. This time around, Sheila was more able to listen to me when I linked these reactions to her self-destructive and self-sabotaging tendencies. Like Richard, Sheila was in one way reluctant to get well. Her sense of having to struggle with deprivation and of being a 'survivor' (but only just a survivor) had become a part of her sense of identity. These entrenched elements stood in opposition to her intelligence and resilience, her courage in naming feelings and experiences, and her determination to move on. At this time, any form of self-care was a real achievement, the winning of a round against envy, self-sabotage and self-destruction. I made sure that Sheila knew that I recognised this.

By the beginning of the third year of therapy, the psychoanalytic environment had enabled Sheila to make a significant shift from punishing and starving her body to responding to her physical needs in a kindly way. At the start, she had been dependent upon me to show care for her and to express concern for her welfare. By now, she had internalised these experiences to the extent that she was able to offer herself a better quality of self-care outside the consulting room.

Seven years of therapy, with sessions three times a week for about a half of that period, may seem a very long treatment to some readers. For somebody like Sheila, who had been deprived of maternal care from the age of twelve and who had come close to destroying herself, I think that it may be the only way to recover properly. As the end of our time together drew closer, Sheila initiated a re-assessment of her early care. She brought in photographs of her mother and showed them to me, pointing out to me how beautiful her mother was and how tenderly she held Sheila as a baby. It had taken seven years of therapy to make accessible the original experience of good enough care that Sheila had enjoyed in infancy.

In terms of my particular theme in this book, I will finish this account by returning to the matter of Sheila's internalisation of my kind and concerned attitude towards her use of the body. My alert interest in Sheila's swimming was in part helpful because it revived for her a sense of her mother's enjoyment of her physicality:

> The baby takes for granted all the things like the softness of the clothes and having the bath water at just the right temperature. What cannot be taken for granted is the mother's pleasure that goes with the clothing and bathing of her own baby. If you are there enjoying it all, it is like the sun coming out for the baby. The mother's pleasure has to be there or else the whole procedure is dead, useless, and mechanical. (Winnicott, 1949b: 27)

## The cultural context of physical exercise

In early human societies, the physical dimension of living was very much to the fore. Energetic physical activities – hunting, digging for roots, chopping wood and building fires – were the very stuff of survival. Even after the Industrial Revolution, most men did manual work of one sort or another. Most women dealt with the physical demands of heavy chores, such as sweeping, scrubbing and washing laundry by hand. The majority of journeys, whether social or work related, were made by bicycle or on foot.

It is not my intention to idealise the lifestyle of previous genera-tions. It was certainly hard, too hard for many people in the lower echelons of society, for whom death was hastened by exhaustion and overwork. Physical work did, however, have the advantage of sustaining a sense of indwelling, of supporting that particular aspect of a sense of identity that comes from feeling properly embodied.

With the development of electronic communications, we have arrived at a situation in which more and more tasks can be performed while sitting at a desk. When we leave the home, our physical exercise may be limited to the walk from the front door to the car. To what extent can most of us still say that we *automatically* experience the full range our physicality in the context of our daily lives? Unless we make a conscious effort to change the situation, many of us will never experience the changes in breathing and heart rate brought on by vigorous exercise, or know the feeling of a muscle aching from exertion.

The effects of a sedentary lifestyle have been very much in the news as far as the physical aspects of health are concerned. We are probably all aware of the increased incidence of obesity and its associated health risks, on both sides of the Atlantic. In contrast, the effects on the *psychological* aspects of health have not been much discussed, yet I believe they are equally important. Winnicott implies that using ourselves physically is one of the ways in which we know ourselves. If we accept this point of view, we might specu-late that this era in Western civilisation provides a perfect context for a poor quality of psychosomatic indwelling, as physical exertion threatens to drop out of our lives entirely.

It is against this background that we need to consider the current 'fitness craze'. An increasing number of people programme into their week regular swimming or gym sessions, or join a yoga class, or take up another leisure exercise or sporting activity. For many people, these activities are a valid expression of a need to redress an imbalance. They represent a psychologically healthy adjustment to the changes that have evolved. In such circumstances, the vigorous use of the body often emerges as complementary to thoughtfulness and the process of symbolisation, involving a coming together of action, thinking and feeling.

In each of its various manifestations, exercise calls for skill, physical coordination and complex movement, as well as for strength. Whether we have in mind a sporting activity, a dance step or an aerobics exercise, it is clear that the learning process involves a progression from gross and approximate movements to precise and well-timed ones. Linking these processes to Esther Bick's work, one could speak in terms of a refining rather than a toughening of the skin.

A growing sense of competence stands alongside the experience of 'sensual muscularity', cited by Richards (1994) in relation to playing football, but presumably also applicable to climbing a stiff hill, holding a yoga position for a little longer or sweating over a weights machine in the gym. Exercise puts us more fully in touch with our physicality. Our breathing becomes more laboured. Our hearts beat faster. Proprioception is brought more keenly into play. We feel our exertions in our torso and in our limbs.

We will no doubt continue to encounter situations where physical exercise is being used in a defensive manner or coming more centrally into the service of pathological functioning. In particular, it may form an aspect of a toughened 'second skin', impairing a person's quality of relationship and exerting a negative effect on the operation of thoughtfulness and imagination. In these situations, it will emerge that the exercising body is not being experienced as 'indwelt' or 'inhabited'. Instead, it is being worked and managed as if it were a machine. We may become aware of such a situation via verbal descriptions of the engagement with exercise, via somatic countertransference experiences, or both.

Sometimes, as in the case of Betty, beneficial and pathological tendencies can be seen in operation within the scenario. If the therapist recognises the situation, he or she is in a position to facilitate a process of transformation, encouraging creative possibilities to come to the fore. The process of talking about exercise activities in psychotherapy is in itself a kind of 'joining up' of the physical and the psychological. As such, it tends to bring the more destructive possibilities of exercise within safe bounds.

I think that most of us would be inclined to assume that a physical activity such as dance will be imaginatively used, while something more mundane, for example taking a step class, might turn out to have more of a 'dead, mechanical and useless' quality. The research I have undertaken to date (see Turp, 2000) has, however, produced results that conflict with these assumptions. It seems that it is not possible to distinguish in a general way between forms of exercise that are likely to be used creatively and those which are likely to be used destructively. Because we are creatures of association and imagination, even an activity such as walking on a treadmill, which appears from the outside mindless, tedious and psychologically useless, may be linked in the inner world to a vision of a forthcoming walking holiday in green hills and dales. In arriving at an evaluation, there is no substitute for clinical experience, when used in the service of gauging an individual client's quality of engagement with a particular exercise activity at a particular time.

Within a dualistic framework, exercise activities have been seen as belonging to the separate realm of the body and therefore as not being of inherent psychological interest. As we shift to a holistic perspective and cease to think in terms of separate 'body' and 'mind' entities, we can reflect on such activities in the context of our overall functioning and consider anew their history, their meanings and our associations to them.

# CHAPTER 12

# Body Storylines

> The live body, with its limits, and with an inside and an outside is felt by the individual to form the core for the imaginative self. (Winnicott, 1949a: 244)

*The concept of a 'body storyline' offers a conceptual framework for thinking about how a person comes to inhabit, experience, make use of, express and narrate his or her 'live body'. In this chapter, I continue to explore the characteristics and meanings of physical 'showings' and narrated 'tellings', and to consider the relationship between them.*

## The 'storying' of experience

I recently turned on my car radio and happened to hear a programme in which a journalist was accompanying a coffee expert in the activity of tasting and evaluating coffees from different parts of the world. When the journalist confessed to 'not being able to tell the difference' between two offerings, the expert described a process of refining both his sense of taste and his language, which had taken place over many years. Essentially, the expert had tasted many, many different coffees, developed a vocabulary for what he tasted and then, with this enlarged vocabulary at his disposal, had become able to distinguish more and more nuances of coffee taste and quality. This, then, is the story of the 'storying' of coffee over the years.

Working with body storylines is something that we all do to some degree. All of us respond unconsciously to a person's appearance, posture, way of walking, way of speaking and so on. Many psychotherapists also attend consciously to these matters and take them into account when thinking about and working with a client.

Susie Orbach summarises the contemporary situation in psychoanalytic psychotherapy:

> The psychotherapist takes body clues into account as he or she assesses whether they can be helpful to a prospective patient. But if the psychotherapist works mainly through 'the talking cure', even though the body is noted, it will not necessarily be examined within the therapy relationship itself and the feelings that are aroused at a physical level within the therapy may be disregarded or the therapist may lack a way to think about them. (Orbach, 1995: 4)

If we initially 'lack a way to think about' these matters, we can nevertheless refine our art through our close attention to client narratives of physicality and, more importantly, to our own physical experience of being in the room with a particular client. In this way, we open ourselves up to the different ways in which body storylines are expressed. Subsequently, we engage in the process of finding words for our experiences. With the refinement of vocabulary comes an enhanced sensitivity to cues in the client narrative and to unconscious somatic communications. Attention to the physically experienced quality of being in the room with a client is always important; in the early stages of the work, we may learn a great deal more from this general feel of things than from a client's verbal self-account.

Psychoanalytic writing on 'alexithymia' (from the Greek, meaning 'not having words for feelings') includes the idea that an absence of words for feelings and physical sensations reflects a situation in which *bodily sensations are themselves reduced or seriously distorted*. As a body storyline unfolds, a clear link may emerge between a client's sense of disconnection and alexithymic tendencies and the management of trauma through the defence of psychosomatic splitting. The following extract from my work with 'Geoffrey' illustrates this situation:

*Geoffrey:* I remember when I was much younger, sitting at the top of the stairs. My father was arguing with my brother who had stayed out quite late. They started to fight, and the glass in the front door got smashed. I think Martin did it. I thought he'd had it then. I was absolutely terrified.

*Maggie:* What did you do?

*Geoffrey:* I sat there, knowing it would be the end of me if they saw me. I remember kind of freezing, stopping breathing, willing them not to look up. But I couldn't tear myself away and go back to my bedroom either. I was kind of transfixed. My mother brought it to a halt. She said to Martin, 'Get up to your room' or something like that, and then to my father, 'We don't want the whole street knowing our business.'

It is interesting that when a process of splitting is remembered and described directly, as it is here, the narrative frequently includes accounts of holding the breath and/or becoming immobile. I have come to think that some of the psychologically restorative potential of physical exercise resides in the vigorous movements involved in the activity and in the consequent freeing up of breathing. Also significant is the sense of the exerciser reclaiming his or her power and ability to act. There are elements here of a manic defence, involving feelings of triumph and omnipotent control, as described by Segal (1981). At the same time, we must be careful not to overlook the valid and essentially healthy enjoyment of the new powers that the exerciser may experience.

In a thoughtful discussion of despair, manic activity and reparation, child psychotherapist Ann Alvarez has written about the importance of new achievements and of a 'valuing of self' for her young clients:

> Such discoveries of a new self should not be confused with pathological narcissism or with states marked by envy and contempt. The children may want, at such moments, not to show off their new achievements but to show and share them. (Alvarez, 1992: 135)

Alvarez goes on to argue that the therapist needs to acknowledge the renewal of hope being expressed by the elated client, rather than focusing prematurely or exclusively on the loss and despair that is being defended against. In my view, the same considerations apply to work with adult clients who come to a session full of enthusiasm about their new dance class or yoga group.

## 'Showings' and 'tellings'

I return here to the work of the American psychoanalyst Roy Schafer, particularly to the valuable distinction he makes between 'showings' (expressive movements and lifestyle choices) and 'tellings' (narratives delivered in a verbal form):

> For example, to say 'I told myself to get going' is to tell a self-story with two characters, an admonishing self and an admonished self. ...And smacking one's head after making a mistake is to make a show of punishing a dumb self. This last example makes it plain that some of these versions of self are non-verbal. That is, they are versions that are shown in expressive movements or life-style rather than told verbally. (Schafer, 1992: 27)

The idea that a story is both shown and told, and that we perceive and respond to both of these aspects of the narrative, is central to the concept of body storylines. 'Showings' are fundamental and always present in some form while 'tellings' are optional. Not every showing needs to be 'storied', to be thought about and translated into a verbal narrative.

From early in life, 'showings' appear in an individual's physical style, posture, energy level and susceptibility to illness. The infant observations presented in Part II reveal some of the ways in which showings are shaped by personal experience, particularly by early experiences of maternal handling. Over the life span, body storylines continue to be played out physically, to be 'shown' and 're-shown'. They may also be 'told' and 're-told' in many different versions, as our experiences in the present and our understandings of the past shift and change. Some experiences, particularly those which are especially joyful, traumatic or familiar, seem to leave a lasting physical inscription. They become permanent, if unmeasurable, aspects of our self-experience and of our unconscious communication with others. Others leave only a temporary mark and are erased by later experience.

The many ways in which unexamined traumatic material can find expression in the form of a 'showing' are well documented in the psychoanalytic literature. There may be a body memory, conscious or unconscious, a particular style of physical self-representation, psychosomatic symptoms or an incomprehensible action or set of rituals. In one very striking example, Dawn Collins has written about a young woman who repeatedly scratched two patches on either side of her neck until they were raw and bleeding. Through looking at the patient's medical records, a member of the hospital staff discovered that the patient had suffered several attempts at strangulation. These strangulation attempts were not consciously remembered by the patient, although she was vaguely able to recollect something of the kind when the issue was raised with her by staff. Collins comments:

> It is as if the trauma, despite the split-off affect and memory, remains located and inscribed in the body. (Collins, 1996: 470)

Similar examples abound in psychoanalytic accounts of psychosomatic illness.

Where showings take the form of psychosomatic symptoms of self-destructive behaviour, bringing a telling into being is the key to change:

> Psychoanalysis is conducted as a dialogue. However much the analyst may remain silent as she or he listens patiently for suitable opportunities to define themes of unconscious conflict, the process still qualifies as dialogue, for each of the analyst's utterances and meaningful silences counts heavily in the course of the work – sometimes far too heavily owing to the influence of powerful transferences. In this dialogue, actions and happenings (for example traumatic events) are continuously being told by the analysand and sooner or later retold interpretively by both analyst and analysand. Closure is always provisional to allow for further retellings. In many instances the tellings are nonverbal enactments: showings that are yet to be transformed into tellings. (Schafer, 1992: xv)

Once a 'telling' is available to be thought about, then the process of bringing meaning to experience has begun, and the possibility of transformation is being actualised.

The situation in health and in everyday living is somewhat different, as there is no pressing need for showings to be 'transformed into tellings'. Nevertheless, the experiences which have enabled us to feel loved and self-confident are reflected in showings – in posture, in facial expression, in general health and vigour. And, as we grow older, body storylines *may* also appear as tellings, in the things we say about ourselves, such as 'I'm not bad at sport' or 'I've always been clumsy.' Some tellings relate specifically to the physical enjoyment that is characteristic of psychosomatic health. I wrote earlier about the six-year-old who said he loved his mother 'because she lets me climb on the shed'. On one occasion, 'Sheila' told me with great feeling, 'You know, I just *love* to swim.' My husband and his sister used to play tennis as children and teenagers. He has described to me how they would scrutinise the weather forecast each day and hope desperately for a fine weekend. 'We dreaded the prospect of a rainy Sunday. It was just about the worst thing we could imagine.' As adults, we sometimes forget the passion associated with physical activities in childhood.

Thus, experiences of childhood handling and adult self-handling, whether sustaining or damaging, are inscribed into a person's posture, level of vitality, physical style, choice of activity (or inactivity) and overall behaviour. Some of those experiences also become a part of that person's narrative of self. In cases of distress and disturbance, the creation of such a 'telling' is essential to the process of making sense of the 'showing' and to the possibility of change. In health, showings may or may not emerge also as tellings. They play their own part in sustaining a sense of individual being and are an important, albeit often silent, aspect of the individual's body storyline.

## Winnicott and body storylines

Our engagement, or non-engagement, with touch and movement activities is always invested with meanings of one kind or another. These meanings relate both to our past experiences and to our current and future visions of ourselves. Our relationship to them is part of a body storyline that begins tentatively as we tumble and turn in the womb and gets properly into its stride as we elicit, negotiate and incorporate our early experiences of handling. The storyline continues with various achievements in the area of physical competence – crawling, walking, running and perhaps eventually climbing a mountain or performing a dance.

Winnicott's writing on the psyche-soma is particularly helpful in thinking about these matters, offering as it does a neutral starting position where physical activities are neither idealised nor denigrated. It offers a basic template for thinking about the vicissitudes of body storylines. According to Winnicott's account, the infant needs to be allowed to live in his or her body, needs not to be called upon to think too much. The 'good enough' mother recognises this and protects her infant from:

> coincidences and other phenomena that must be beyond the infant's ability to comprehend. (Winnicott, 1963: 86)

In unfavourable circumstances, a split between psyche and soma aspects of the self is threatened. Winnicott saw psychosomatic symptoms as evidence both of the split itself and of an unconscious endeavour to redeem the unity of the psyche-soma:

> We can see that one of the aims of psychosomatic illness is to draw the psyche from the mind back to the original intimate association with the soma. (1949a: 254)

Like most psychoanalysts, Winnicott worked with many patients who suffered from serious and sometimes life-threatening psychosomatic illnesses. I have decided to keep the focus in this book, as far as is possible, on health and everyday living. I acknowledge, however, that for some unfortunate individuals, negative experiences have had an overriding effect. The narratives presented in the previous chapters give an idea of the potential value of thinking in terms of body storylines with clients who have suffered from emotional, physical or sexual abuse. I hope to be able to explore this theme at greater length in the future.

## Essentially physical activities

I have suggested that, in health, engagement with essentially physical activities tends towards the enhancement or recovery of a good quality of psychosomatic indwelling. The activity supports and complements the expression of the 'imaginative self', referred to by Winnicott in the quotation that begins this chapter. In these circumstances, there is a sense of action, thinking and feeling coming together. The composer Benjamin Britten, for example, is known to have taken long 'thinking walks' when he ran short of musical inspiration. Other people go to the gym, or practise t'ai chi, or swim, or play a game of football in order to enter what might be described as a meditative space. Logical, deductive thinking is switched off for a while, and the mental batteries have an opportunity to recharge. Some of us find that new ideas arise in the space that is created. In one of the rare television programmes on this subject, a vicar interviewed on a running machine in a gym averred that all his best ideas for sermons came to him while he was running!

The sense of enhanced psychosomatic indwelling – that I am my body and that my body is me – which follows on in benign circumstances from a massage or a period of exercise also has profound implications for emotional functioning:

> Without anatomy, emotions do not exist. Feelings have a somatic architecture. (Keleman, 1985: xii)

Essentially, physical activities enhance somatic awareness, and good enough somatic awareness is in turn essential to our contact with our own 'gut feelings' and to our sensitivity to the feelings of others. Emma's changed appearance, arising in part from her ability to use crawling and walking in the service of enhancing her relationship with her mother, is a good example of 'showing' that is suffused with emotional elements. Emma becomes more lively and vigorous, less pale and runny-nosed. At the same time, she becomes much more active in her relationship with her mother and also more interested in interacting with the observer. She is now receptive and communicative, and her facial expressions and bodily gestures show that she is fully emotionally present.

In psychoanalytic psychotherapy with adults, the creative use of essentially physical activities can emerge in the form of both showings and tellings. Showings take the form of physical change, which finds an infinite number of different kinds of expression. Sometimes there is just a general sense of more energy and openness. Sometimes a more specific change, such as a new hair-style, may make an impression on the therapist. The situation is clarified when a telling comes into being alongside the showing. Where activities are being used creatively, the telling is likely to include thoughtful client descriptions of what it feels like to engage in the activity and to be amenable to a wide range of memories, feelings and associations.

On the other hand, the pathological use of essentially physical activities is associated with the numbing and splitting that are characteristic of the 'duality psyche-soma', seen by Winnicott as expressing an extreme and defensive split between mental and physical aspects of the self. Again, this situation will usually be evident in showings, often before it is described verbally. The client may be dirty or unkempt, be dressed in a summer frock in the middle of winter or look exhausted. The tone of voice is flat. He or she moves stiffly or is very static. The atmosphere feels rather dead. There is very little 'spark' in the interaction, whether silent or spoken, and sessions may feel like very hard work.

If a corresponding telling appears, it may include narratives of calorie-counting or of an obsessional adherence to an exercise programme. Descriptions of 'not feeling real', of psychosomatic symptoms, of eating problems and of self-neglect or self-injury all reflect psychosomatic splitting. The client may let the therapist know how dissociated she feels by referring to her bodily self as a 'not me' item, as an object viewed from the outside. In this case, the body may be cared for in a cosmetic and mechanical way, but there is no real sense of indwelling or inhabitation. Faced with tellings of this kind, we need to be particularly alert to the manner in which essentially physical activities are being used (or not being avoided) if they are mentioned during the course of therapy.

It sometimes becomes clear that the client engages in virtually no physical activity, that profound physical inertia is part of the overall pathology. Where physical activity is described, there is a risk that it is characteristic of handling/self-handling which Winnicott describes as 'dead, mechanical and useless'. On the other hand, the activity may represent a bid for recovery. In my experience, a non-judgmental exploration of the meanings behind the activity is very worthwhile. In some cases, I think it has ensured that the healthy rather than the pathological tendencies folded into the exercise activity are those which have come to fruition.

## Unconscious somatic communication

The therapist's use of her body is an extension of the 'use of self' widely being discussed within contemporary psychoanalysis, particularly in the work of the social constructivitists and the interpersonalists. (Orbach, 1995: 3)

Susie Orbach points out that neither Margaret Mahler nor Joyce McDougall, both of whom who have written extensively on psychosomatic issues, refers to countertransferential feelings. 'Listening with the body' is a continuous implicit theme in the infant observation extracts and case histories that I have presented. As theory in this area is in the relatively early stages of development, however, I will offer some additional comments and examples. For readers who are interested in exploring this subject further, I recommend the work of Susie Orbach, of Nathan Field and of the Jungian analyst Marilyn Matthew.

At the most general level, some clients give us energy and others drain us. With experience, we can tell that this is their impact upon us rather than a mood we bring with us into the consulting room. The client's effect on our energetic state can be regarded as an unconscious communication, registered in a visceral way. Each therapist's body is his or her own instrument, and each of us registers somatic communications in a personal and individual way. Below, I offer some examples drawn from my own practice and from supervision sessions with other counsellors and psychotherapists. Some of the situations described echo those which were featured in the longer case studies presented in Chapters 10 and 11.

1. Some clients adopt a 'reporting' style of (non-)engagement. What they say is intellectually coherent, but they seem to be reading from a text prepared prior to arriving in the room. The tone tends to be rather flat. It is easy to be misled, since such clients will often bring interesting material relating to relationships or dreams. But the sense in the room is of a 'talking head' with an inert or absent body. The client may be physically very still. Possible clues in the countertransference are a wish to sleep, physical discomfort and a desire *not to hear*, to switch off the client's voice.

2. A client may speak with a more normal degree of animation but communicate something unspoken in his or her appearance. He or she may come over as vulnerable, wispy or neglected, perhaps through a slight dishevelment or through wearing clothes that are far too warm or far too flimsy for the weather and the season. The narrative often speaks of indecision and a sense of helplessness. Such a client sometimes reveals that she

is finding it very difficult to take care of herself, particularly in sexual relationships, where she may be being exploited or abused. My countertransference responses have included a strong urge to hold the client physically, a tendency to see the client as being much younger than she actually is, and fleeting images of providing a healthy and hearty meal or a set of warm comfortable clothes.

3. A client comes and engages in a warm and intelligent way. She is sociable and apparently appreciative of what she gets in therapy. The narrative includes frequent descriptions of physical ills, ranging from unexplained aches and pains to headaches to extreme fatigue to food allergies. It is difficult to think here in terms of 'countertransference feelings', since these are noticeable mainly by their absence. The therapist eventually becomes aware of having no 'gut feeling' at all for what is going on. In this false self, or in Orbach's terms 'false body' presentation, there is a pressing invitation to relate at a rather superficial social level and a tacit resistance to any disturbance of the client's prepared account.

4. Some clients have a physical self-presentation that speaks of being 'mistreated but tough'. Leather jackets are common (although I am not suggesting that wearing a leather jacket automatically places a client in this category!). There may be a great deal of resentment in the client's tone of voice. A punitive relationship to the body may be evident in scarring, in extreme thinness or in descriptions of situations where the client seems to court violence or injury. In the countertransference, the therapist may find him or herself sitting very upright, adhering to a rather 'proper' technique and being particularly strict about keeping time. On examination, these tendencies may be linked to a feeling of threat and of potential attack.

## Working with body storylines

Essentially, working with body storylines involves the narration and re-narration of events that have centrally involved a person's experience and use of physicality. The task of enabling a client to join up the physiological with the psychological, to make links between 'self-handling' activities undertaken outside the consulting room and his or her history and present state of being has been considered through the presentation and discussion of specific clinical examples.

Working with body storylines is a part of the overall process of psychoanalytic psychotherapy. Indeed, it is crucial that working with a body storyline is not seen as a separate enterprise. The aim of psychosomatic integration is unlikely to be well served by any compartmentalised consideration of touch and movement activities. Instead, a consideration of the changing experiences of physicality over the years of living and the months of psychotherapy needs to be integrated with the consideration of other issues – relationship difficulties, issues of personal creativity, difficulties in making decisions or whatever else the client brings to the sessions. The principle of 'being with' rather than 'doing to' holds firm. In special cases (for example, when working with children), art drama or play therapy may form a part of the proceedings, but even here the focus is on 'being with', on the shifting quality of the therapist–client relationship, rather than on the activity itself.

Thus, the ordinary, careful elucidation of possible meanings of a particular communication proceeds with reference to issues in the transference and to countertransference emotions, thoughts, sensations and intuitions. Beyond this, the selection of body storylines for particular consideration calls for a close attention to three sources of information.

The first is any notable change in one's own posture, breathing or physical stance. As I have pointed out, we often unconsciously echo aspects of another person's physical posture and style, particularly when, as in therapy, we wish to understand their unique experience of being in the world. Our own physical way of being in the presence of a particular client is therefore a potentially useful source of information. Closely linked to these postural mirrorings and our reflections upon them are other kinds of embodied countertransference experience – feeling cold, feeling restless, developing a headache and so on – described by Nathan Field (1989) and in the case examples I have presented. Third, the therapist is particularly alert to verbal references to 'essentially physical' experiences and activities, such as playing sport, taking steam baths or massages – or perhaps body-brushing, running, swimming and deliberately colliding with other people!

As practitioners whose work is founded in psychoanalytic ideas, we strive to maintain a state of 'evenly suspended attention' (Freud, 1912). At the same time, we understand that we bring certain belief systems and sensitivities into the consulting room and that these influence what we hear, what we make of what we hear and which aspects of a client narrative are chosen for elaboration. One of my own beliefs is that the body has a rightful place in the expression and management of feelings. I think a sense of being properly embodied is fundamental to a satisfactory experience of living.

Not surprisingly, my preoccupation with physical self-expression and its many meanings has made me particularly sensitive to any lack of harmony between physical and verbal aspects of functioning. In this sense, I am one of the 'coffee experts' of subtle physical communication. I often discern in a client's physical self-presentation an unconscious request for help with the task of restoring psychosomatic harmony, a request that is later confirmed in his or her verbal narrative. White and Epston (1990) have described a narrative as always containing an 'excess of data'; we must inevitably select some aspects of client communication for detailed consideration and let others pass by. Sometimes I find it useful to select a body storyline for further elaboration, even when this means that other possible avenues are left unexplored.

Although I have focused on client narratives involving descriptions of touch and movement experiences and activities, the opportunity to pick up on a body storyline is not limited to these situations. Some time ago, a client who had been feeling very low arrived ten minutes late and said, 'I almost didn't come today. It was so very difficult to get out of bed.' I could have remarked on the client's mixed feelings about coming, or referred back to a difficult previous session or to a recent occasion when I had cancelled our appointment. Instead, I followed the body storyline and said 'You found it a real struggle to get out of bed?' In this way, I registered my interest in the client's physical experience and implicitly invited her to say more about it. At the back of my mind were questions about what associations 'bed' has for this client and about what this struggle to rise was like for her. I had a hunch that this client if she just once felt energetic and sprang out of her bed would tell me about it. In fact, she did tell me something along these lines quite a lot later. At that time, we were able to recognise this very physically felt shift as a sign of change, a precursor to a fuller recovery which was still some way off. When a client is struggling to hold on to hope, a recognition and acknowledgement of such moments can be very significant.

## Concluding thoughts

In *The Water in the Glass*, Nick Totton expresses a wish that I wholeheartedly share:

> to redress a balance which has swayed too far towards the hegemony of 'mind'; to restore to our awareness the equal centrality of 'body'. (1998: 8)

Totton engages with this imbalance through revisiting the work of Wilhelm Reich and Sandor Ferenczi. My own endeavour to restore the equal centrality of the body builds on the work of Winnicott and on the description and theory emerging from the practice of psychoanalytic infant observation.

Each line of development has its particular strengths, and, as always, there is room for more than one point of view. The depiction of fixed developmental stages (whether Freudian or Reichian) speaks of a concrete reality, a solid and definable set of situations and a cause and effect sequence of events that is inimical to the narrative perspective which I have embraced. The account I offer is shaped both by contemporary object relations theory and by the postmodern emphasis on the shifting and constantly re-narrated nature of human experience.

I have suggested that the informal association between psychoanalysis and narrative is inherent in the subject matter under discussion – the telling of a story, whether by a client in psychoanalytic psychotherapy or by an observer engaged in the practice of psychoanalytic infant observation. Bringing a narrative framework formally into relationship with Winnicott's concept of 'the psyche indwelling in the soma' brings into focus the client's 'body storyline'. The shape of the body storyline, as it becomes clearer, speaks in equal measure of the environment that the individual has encountered, of his or her interpretation and use of that environment, and of the wider cultural context within which these individual elements are embedded. The number of ways in which the processes described can be played out is infinite. Each of us shows in actions and tells in words a unique and specific body storyline.

For a body storyline to be of use to the individual, it needs to feel authentic, to feel like a personal truth. A good quality of indwelling, a feeling of groundedness in physicality, is the backbone of what Winnicott called a 'continuity of going-on-being'. I have argued that it is our ongoing physical self-experience that gives us a sense of stability, an ever-present opportunity to 'touch base'. In health, each of us might say, 'My body has changed in many ways since I was an infant but it remains "my body". It is fundamental to my experience of me.'

# Bibliography

Abram, J. (1996) *The Language of Winnicott*. London: Karnac.

Ainsworth, M. (1969) Object relations, dependency and attachment: a theoretical review of the infant–mother relationship. *Child Development*, **40**: 969–1025.

Alexander, F. (1950) *Psychosomatic Medicine: Its Principles and Applications*. New York: W.W. Norton.

Alvarez, A. (1992) *Live Company*. London: Routledge.

Arnold, L. (1995) *Women and Self-injury – a Survey of 76 Women*. Bristol Crisis Service for Women, P.O. Box 654, Bristol BS99 1XH.

Austen, J. (1811) *Sense and Sensibility*. Oxford: Oxford University Press (1980).

Bakal, D. (1999) *Minding the Body: Clinical Uses of Somatic Awareness*. New York: Guilford Press.

Barnard, K.E. and Brazelton, T.B. (eds) (1990) *Touch: The Foundation of Experience*. Connecticut: IUP.

Baudrillard, J. (1995) *Simulacra and Simulation (The Body in Theory: Histories of Cultural Materialism)*, trans. S. Faria Glaser. Ann Arbor, MI: University of Michigan Press.

Berger, B. and Owen, D. (1992) Mood alteration with yoga and swimming. *Perceptual and Motor Skills*, **75**: 1331–4.

Berger, B., Friedmann, R. and Eaton, M. (1988) Comparison of jogging, relaxation response and group interaction for stress reduction. *Journal of Sport and Exercise Psychology*, **10**: 431–7.

Bermudez, J.L., Marcel, A. and Eilan, N. (eds) (1995) *The Body and The Self*. Cambridge, MA: MIT Press.

Bick, E. (1968) The experience of the skin in early object relations. *International Journal of Psychoanalysis*, **49**: 484–6.

Bion, W.R. (1962) *Learning from Experience*. London: Heinemann.

Blackmer Dexter, J. (1989) *The Acrobats of the Gods*. Toronto: Inner City Books.

Boadella, D. (1998) Quality of life: the matrix of transformation and the frontiers of psychotherapy. *European Journal of Psychotherapy, Counselling and Health*, **1**(2): 257–69.

Bollas, C. (1987) *The Shadow of the Object*. London: Free Association Books.

Bollas, C. (1993) *Being a Character*. London: Routledge.

Boss, M. (1963) *Psychoanalysis and Daseinanalysis,* trans. I.B. Lefèbre. New York: Basic Books.

Bower, T.G.R. (1977) *A Primer in Infant Development.* San Francisco: Freeman.

Bower, T. (1989) The perceptual world of the newborn child. In Slater, A. and Bremner, G. (eds) *Infant Development.* Hove: Lawrence Erlbaum Associates.

Bowlby, J. (1988) *A Secure Base.* London: Routledge.

Bradley, B. (1989) *Visions of Infancy: A Critical Introduction to Child Psychology.* Cambridge: Polity Press.

Brazelton, T. (1975) *Infants and Mothers.* New York: Delacourt Press.

Bridge, G. and Miles, G. (eds) (1996) *On the Outside Looking in – Collected Essays on Young Child Observation in Social Work Training.* London: CCETSW.

Briggs, S. (1997) *Growth and Risk in Infancy.* London: Jessica Kingsley.

Broom, B. (1997) *Somatic Illness and the Patient's Other Story.* London: Free Association Books.

Burr, V. (1995) *An Introduction to Social Constructionism.* London: Routledge.

Byng-Hall, J. (1995) *Reviewing Family Scripts: Improvisation and Systems Change.* London: Guilford.

Cardinal, M. (1993) *The Words To Say it.* London: Women's Press.

Casement, P. (1982) Some pressures on the analyst for physical contact during the re-living of an early trauma. *International Review of Psycho-Analysis,* **9**: 279–86.

Collins, D. (1996) Attacks on the body: how can we understand self-harm? *Psychodynamic Counselling,* **2**(4): 463–75.

Damasio, A. (1994) *Descartes' Error: Emotion, Reason and the Human Brain.* New York: Putman.

Damasio, A. (1999) *The Feeling of What Happens: Body and Emotion in the Making of Consciousness.* London: Heinemann.

De la Torre, J. (1995) Mens sana in corpore sano, or exercise abuse? *Bulletin of the Menninger Clinic,* **59**: 15–27.

Denzin, N.K. (1970) *The Research Act.* Chicago: Aldine.

Descartes, R. (1644) *Principles of Philosophy,* trans. E. Anscombe and P. Geach (1954). London: Nelson.

Edelman, G. (1992) *Bright Air, Brilliant Fire.* New York: Basic Books.

Eiden, B. (1998) The use of touch in psychotherapy. *Self and Society,* **26**: 1–3.

Elliott, A. and Frosh, S. (1995) *Psychoanalysis in Contexts: Paths Between Theory and Modern Culture.* London: Routledge.

Favazza, A. (1989a) Normal and deviant self-mutilation: an essay review. *Transcultural Psychiatric Research Review,* **26**(2): 113–27.

Favazza, A. (1989b) Why patients mutilate themselves. *Hospital and Community Psychiatry,* **40**(2): 137–45.

Field, N. (1989) Listening with the body: an exploration in the counter-transference. *British Journal of Psychotherapy*, **5**(4): 512–22.

Field, T.M. (ed.) (1995) *Touch in Early Development*. Hillsdale, NJ: Lawrence Erlbaum Associates.

Foucault, M. (1984) Space, knowledge and power. In Rabinow, P. (ed.) *The Foucault Reader*. New York: Pantheon.

Fox, N. (1999) *Beyond Health: Postmodernism and Embodiment*. London: Free Association Books.

Freedman, J. and Combs, G. (1996) *Narrative Therapy*. New York: W.W. Norton.

Freud, S. (1891) Monograph on aphasia. In *Standard Edition*, Vol. 14. London: Hogarth.

Freud, S. (1895) On hysteria. In *Standard Edition*, Vol. 2. London: Hogarth.

Freud, S. (1911) Formulations on the two principles of mental func-tioning. In *Standard Edition*, Vol. 12. London: Hogarth.

Freud, S. (1912) Papers on technique. In *Standard Edition*, Vol. 12. London: Hogarth.

Freud, S. (1916) Fixation to traumas – the unconscious. In *Standard Edition*, Vol. 16. London: Hogarth.

Freud, S. (1923) The ego and the id. In *Standard Edition*, Vol. 18. London: Hogarth.

Freud, S. and Breuer, J. (1893) Studies in hysteria. In *Standard Edition*, Vol. 2. London: Hogarth.

Groddeck G. (1977) *The Meaning of Illness*. London: Hogarth.

Harlow, H.F. and Harlow, M.K. (1962) Social deprivation in monkeys. *Scientific American*, **207**: 136–44.

Harris, M. (1978) Towards learning from experience. In Harris Williams, M. (ed.) *Collected Papers of Martha Harris and Esther Bick*. Perthshire: Clunie.

Heaton, J.M. (1967) Depth. *Confinia Psychiatrica*, **10**: 210–37.

Heaton, J.M. (1993) The sceptical tradition in psychotherapy. In Spurling, L. (ed.) *From the Words of my Mouth: Tradition in Psychotherapy*. London: Tavistock.

Heaton, J. (1998) The enigma of health. *European Journal of Psychotherapy, Counselling and Health*, **1**(1): 33–42.

Heidegger, M. (1927) *Being and Time*, trans. J. Macquarrie and E.S. Robinson (1962). New York: Harper & Row.

Heimann, P. (1952) Notes on the theory of the life and death instincts. In Klein, M., Heimann, P., Isaacs, S. and Rivière, J. (eds) *Developments in Psychoanalysis*. London: Hogarth.

Hoffer, W. (1950) Contribution to the Panel on 'Psychoanalysis and Devel-opmental Psychology', held at the Meeting of the American Psychoana-lytic Association, Detroit, 29 April.

Hopkins, J. (1990) The observed infant of attachment theory. *British Journal of Psychotherapy*, **6**: 457–69.

Howe, D. (1993) *On Being a Client*. London: Sage.

Isaacs, S. (1952) The nature and function of phantasy. In Klein, M., Heinemann, P., Isaacs, S. and Rivière, J. (eds) *Developments in Psychoanalysis*. London: Hogarth.

Jung, C.G. (1933) *Modern Man in Search of a Soul*. London: Routledge.

Jung, C.G. (1956) The symbolic life. In *Collected Works*, Vol. 18. London: Routledge & Kegan Paul.

Jung, C.G. (1963) *Memories, Dreams and Reflections*. London: Collins and Routledge & Kegan Paul.

Keleman S. (1985) *Emotional Anatomy: The Structure of Experience*. Berkeley, CA: Center Press.

Kertay, L. and Reviere, S. (1993) The use of touch in psychotherapy: theoretical and ethical considerations. *Psychotherapy*, **30**(1): 32–40.

Kirschenbaum, H. and Land Henderson, V. (eds) (1990) *Carl Rogers Dialogues*. London: Constable.

Klein, M. (1921) The development of a child. In *Love, Guilt and Reparation and Other Works 1921–1945*. London: Hogarth.

Klein, M. (1946) Notes on some schizoid mechanisms. In Klein, M. (1975) *Envy and Gratitude and Other Works 1946–1963*. London: Hogarth.

Klein, M. (1952) On observing the behaviour of young infants. In *Developments in Psychoanalysis*. London: Hogarth.

Klein, M. (1957) Envy and gratitude. In Klein, M. (1975) *Envy and Gratitude and Other Works 1946–1963*. London: Hogarth.

Kobasa, S., Maddi, S., Puccetti, M. and Zola, M. (1985) The effectiveness of hardiness, exercise and social support as resources against illness. *Journal of Psychosomatic Research*, 29: 525–33.

Kuhn, T. (1962) *The Structure of Scientific Revolutions*. Chicago: University of Chicago Press.

Levinas, E. (1978) *Existence and Existents*, trans. A. Lingis. The Hague: Martinus Nijhoff.

Lewis, M. (ed.) (1991) Child and Adolescent Psychiatry. A Comprehensive Textbook. Baltimore, London: Williams and Wilkins.

Likierman M. (1993) 'He drew my attention to my great capacity for understanding children...' Some thoughts on Sandor Ferenczi and his influence on Melanie Klein. *British Journal of Psychotherapy*, **9**(4): 444–55.

McDougall, J. (1974) The psychosomatic and psycho-analytic process. *International Review of Psychoanalysis*, **1**: 437–54.

McDougall, J. (1989) *Theatres of the Body: A Psychoanalytical Approach to Psychosomatic Illness*. London: Free Association Books.

Marshall, I. and Zohar, D. (1997) *Who's Afraid of Schrödinger's Cat?* London: Bloomsbury.

Maslow, A.H. (1943) A theory of human motivation. *Psychological Review*, **50**: 370–96.

Merleau-Ponty, M. (1962) *Phenomenology of Perception*, trans. C. Smith. London: Routledge & Kegan Paul.

Messer, S. and Warren, C. (1995) *Models of Brief Psychodynamic Therapy: A Comparative Approach*. New York: Guildford Press.

Miller, L., Rustin, M., Rustin, M. and Shuttleworth, J. (eds) (1989) *Closely Observed Infants*. London: Duckworth.

Murray, L. (1988) Effects of post-natal depression on infant development. In Kumar, R. and Brockington, I. (eds) *Motherhood and Mental Illness 2*. London: Wright.

Murray, L. (1989) Winnicott and the developmental psychology of infancy. *British Journal of Psychotherapy*, **5**(3): 333–48.

O'Brien, S. and Conger, P. (1991) No time to look back: approaching the finish line of life's course. *International Journal of Ageing and Human Development*, **33**: 75–87.

Ogden, T. (1997) *Reverie and Interpretation: Sensing Something Human*. Northvale, NJ: Jason Aronson.

Olds, D. and Cooper, A. (1997) Dialogue with other sciences: opportunities for mutual gain. *International Journal of Psychoanalysis*, **78**: 219–25.

Orbach, S. (1995) Countertransference and the false body. In *Winnicott Studies*, **10**: 3–13.

Payne, H. (ed.) (1992) *Dance Movement Therapy: Theory and Practice*. London: Routledge.

Phillips, A. (1988) *Winnicott*. London: Fontana.

Phillips, A. (1993) *On Kissing, Tickling and Being Bored*. London: Faber and Faber.

Phillips, A. (1999) *Darwin's Worms*. London: Basic Books.

Raphael-Leff, J. (1984) Myths and modes of motherhood. *British Journal of Psychotherapy*, **1**: 6–30.

Rayner, E. (1991) *The Independent Mind in British Psychoanalysis*. Northvale, NJ: Jason Aronson.

Reich, W. (1942/1973) *The Function of the Orgasm*. London: Souvenir Press.

Reich, W. (1945/1972) *Character Analysis*. New York: Touchstone.

Reid, S. (1997) The generation of psychoanalytic knowledge: sociological and clinical perspectives. Part two: Projective identification – the other side of the equation. *British Journal of Psychotherapy*, **13**(4): 542–4.

Richards, B. (1994) The glory of the game. In Richards, B. (ed.) *Disciplines of Delight*. London: Free Association Books.

Robertson, J. (1953) *A Two Year Old Goes to Hospital*. Ipswich: Concord Films Council.

Rodman, F. (ed.) (1987) *The Spontaneous Gesture: Selected Letters of D.W. Winnicott*. Cambridge, MA: Harvard.

Rogers, C. (1980) *A Way of Being*. Boston, MA: Houghton Mifflin.

Rose, T. and Loewenthal, D. (1998) A heuristic investigation: is there a need for a counselling/psychotherapy service for people with cleft lips? *European Journal of Psychotherapy, Counselling and Health*, **1**(1): 105–20.

Rustin, M. (1991) *The Good Society and the Inner World: Psychoanalysis, Politics and Culture.* London: Verso.

Rustin, M (1997) The generation of psychoanalytic knowledge: sociological and clinical perspectives. Part one: 'Give me a consulting room...' *British Journal of Psychotherapy*, **13**(4): 527–41.

Rycroft, C. (1991) *Viewpoints.* London: Hogarth Press.

Said, E. (1999) *Out of Place: A Memoir.* New York: Knopf Publications.

Schafer, R. (1992) *Retelling a Life, Narration and Dialogue in Psychoanalysis.* New York: Basic Books.

Segal, H. (1981) *The Work of Hanna Segal: A Kleinian Approach to Clinical Practice.* London: Aronson.

Shaw, F. (1998) *Composing Myself: A Journey through Postpartum Depression.* London: Steerforth Press.

Sheridan, C. and Radmacher, S. (1992) *Health Psychology: Challenging the Biomedical Model.* New York: Wiley.

Sifneos, P.E. (1965) *Ascent from Chaos: A Psychoanalytic Case Study.* London: Oxford University Press.

Soth, M. (1999) The body in counselling. *Counselling News – The Voice of Counselling Training.*

Spinelli, E. (1989) *The Interpreted World: An Introduction to Phenomenological Psychology.* London: Sage.

Spitz, R. (1945) Hospitalism: an inquiry into the genesis of psychiatric conditions in early childhood. *Psychoanalytic Study of the Child*, **1**: 53–74.

Stern, D.N. (1977) *The First Relationship: Infant and Mother.* Cambridge, MA: Harvard University Press.

Stern, D.N. (1985) *The Interpersonal World of the Infant: A View from Psychoanalysis and Developmental Psychology.* New York: Basic Books.

Symington, N. (1986) *The Analytic Experience: Lectures from the Tavistock.* London: Free Association Books.

Totton, N. (1998) *The Water in the Glass: Body and Mind in Psychoanalysis.* London: Rebus.

Trevarthen, C.B. (1979) Communication and cooperation in early infancy: a description of primary intersubjectivity. In Bullowa, M. (ed.) *Before Speech.* Cambridge: Cambridge University Press.

Turp, M. (1997) The role of physical exercise in emotional well-being. *Psychodynamic Counselling*, **3**(2): 165–77.

Turp, M. (1999a) Working with body storylines. *Psychodynamic Counselling*, **5**(3): 301–17.

Turp, M. (1999b) Encountering self-harm in psychotherapy and counselling practice. *British Journal of Psychotherapy*, **15**(3): 306–21.

Turp, M. (2000) Handling and self-handling: an object relations perspective on leisure exercise. In *Psychodynamic Counselling*, **6**(4): 467–86.

Weinberg, R., Burton, D., Yukerson, D. and Weigard, D. (1993) Goal setting in competitive sport. *Sporting Psychologist*, 7: 275–89.

White, M. and Epston, D. (1990) *Narrative Means to Therapeutic Ends*. New York: Norton & Co.

Wilson, C. and Mintz, I. (eds) (1989) *Psychosomatic Symptoms: Psychodynamic Treatment of the Underlying Personality Disorder*. Northvale, NJ: Jason Aronson.

Winnicott, D.W. (1931) *Clinical Notes on Disorders of Childhood*. London: Heinemann.

Winnicott, D.W. (1941) The observation of infants in a set situation. In *Collected Papers: Through Paediatrics to Psychoanalysis* (1958). London: Tavistock.

Winnicott, D.W. (1949a) Mind and its relation to the psyche-soma. In *Collected Papers: Through Paediatrics to Psychoanalysis* (1958). London: Tavistock.

Winnicott, D.W. (1949b) The baby as a going concern. In *The Child and The Family* (1957). London: Tavistock.

Winnicott, D.W. (1953) Transitional objects and transitional phenomena. In *Collected Papers: Through Paediatrics to Psychoanalysis* (1958). London: Tavistock.

Winnicott, D.W. (1960a) Ego distortion in terms of true and false self. In Winnicott, D.W. (1965) *The Maturational Processes and the Facilitating Environment*. London: Hogarth.

Winnicott, D.W. (1960b) The theory of the parent–infant relationship. In Winnicott, D.W. (1965) *The Maturational Processes and the Facilitating Environment*. London: Hogarth.

Winnicott, D.W. (1962) Ego integration in child development. In Winnicott, D.W. (1965) *The Maturational Processes and the Facilitating Environment*. London: Hogarth.

Winnicott, D.W. (1963) From dependence towards independence: in the development of the individual. In Winnicott, D.W. (1965) *The Maturational Processes and the Facilitating Environment*. London: Hogarth.

Winnicott, D.W. (1966) Psychosomatic illness in its positive and negative aspects. *International Journal of Psychoanalysis*, **47**: 510–15.

Winnicott, D.W. (1967) The concept of a healthy individual. In Winnicott, C., Shepherd, R. and Davis, M. (eds) (1986) *Home Is Where We Start From*. London: Penguin.

Winnicott, D.W. (1970) On the basis for self in body. In Winnicott, C., Shepherd, R. and Davis, M. (eds) (1989) *Psychoanalytic Explorations*. London: Karnac.

Winnicott, D.W. (1988) *Human Nature*. London: Free Association Books.

# Index